Migrating to Swift from Web Development

Sean Liao
Mark Punak

Apress®

Migrating to Swift from Web Development

ISBN-13 (pbk): 978-1-4842-0932-5

ISBN-13 (electronic): 978-1-4842-0931-8

Managing Director: Welmoed Spahr
Lead Editor: Michelle Lowman
Editorial Board: Steve Anglin, Gary Cornell, Louise Corrigan, James T. DeWolf, Jonathan Gennick, Robert Hutchinson, Michelle Lowman, James Markham, Matthew Moodie, Jeffrey Pepper, Douglas Pundick, Ben Renow-Clarke, Gwenan Spearing, Matt Wade, Steve Weiss
Coordinating Editor: Kevin Walter
Copy Editor: Kim Wimpsett
Compositor: SPi Global
Indexer: SPi Global
Artist: SPi Global
Cover Image: Michelle Lowman

Distributed to the book trade worldwide by Springer Science+Business Media New York, 233 Spring Street, 6th Floor, New York, NY 10013. Phone 1-800-SPRINGER, fax (201) 348-4505, e-mail orders-ny@springer-sbm.com, or visit www.springeronline.com. Apress Media, LLC is a California LLC and the sole member (owner) is Springer Science + Business Media Finance Inc (SSBM Finance Inc). SSBM Finance Inc is a Delaware corporation.

For information on translations, please e-mail rights@apress.com, or visit www.apress.com.

Apress and friends of ED books may be purchased in bulk for academic, corporate, or promotional use. eBook versions and licenses are also available for most titles. For more information, reference our Special Bulk Sales–eBook Licensing web page at www.apress.com/bulk-sales.

Any source code or other supplementary material referenced by the author in this text is available to readers at www.apress.com. For detailed information about how to locate your book's source code, go to www.apress.com/source-code/.

Contents at a Glance

Contents

About the Author

Sean Liao started his first mobile app on a PalmOS PDA app in 2000. He hasn't missed any major mobile evolutions. He has written mobile code for PalmOS, JavaME, Microsoft .NET CF, and BlackBerry, and he also has some Nokia Symbian experience. He has been a seasoned Java solution architect since 1998.

Currently, Sean is primarily engaged in creating iOS apps and porting them to Android as a bonus.

Acknowledgments

This book is the joint effort of three developers who specialize in different areas. While specializing in native mobile platforms, I don't have enough hands-on experiences in web technologies. Thanks to my old friend, Mark Punak, who started the book project with me. Without his endorsement and early validations, this book would never have gotten started.

Thank you to my colleague, Tony Nemec, who gave me a huge boost. He is always my go-to guy pretty much for everything, from JavaScript programming and CSS to DIY projects in my garage. Without his help, this book would not have gotten to the finish line.

Special thanks to our publisher, who had faith in this topic, and the editors, who never stopped making the book better. Their professional services and guidance were unparalleled. I am really grateful to have had the Apress publishing and editorial teams with me at all times.

Introduction

In 2000, I created my first mobile app for an inventory-tracking project using PalmOS handheld devices. The initial project was a full-staffed team effort that consisted of mobile developers, SAP consultants, supply-chain subject-matter experts, middleware developers, QA testers, architects, business sponsors, and so forth. JavaME came up strong in 2002, followed by Pocket PC/Windows Mobile. I did several mobile projects in which I converted mobile apps to the Pocket PC platform by blindly translating C++ to JavaME to C# .NETCF mobile code. These "translation" efforts prolonged the whole product life cycle. The project achieved a higher return on investment (ROI) by extending the product life because the extra cost of translating mobile code was surprisingly low. Ever since then, I have been translating front-end mobile apps among various mobile platforms. In recent years, most of my work has involved porting mobile apps between Android and iOS and mobilizing existing web sites. Porting apps between iOS and Android is fairly straightforward. This is also true for porting mobile web apps using a RESTful service. Even for traditional non-service-oriented web apps, you still want to follow the same path: reusing existing business cases and software artifacts and reaching a bigger audience to maximize the ROI.

One thing is for sure: there are a lot demands for mobilizing existing web apps to reach mobile users. That's why I decided to write this book.

The primary objective of this book is to help experienced web developers leap into native iOS–Swift mobile development. It is easier than you think, and this book will make it even easier with step-by-step guidelines. You can immediately translate common mobile use cases to iOS.

Who Is This Book For?

This book was specifically written for web developers who want to make iOS mobile apps. The book will show you the common iOS programming subjects and frameworks by relating them to your familiar web programming tasks when appropriate.

How This Book Is Organized

In part I, you will get the iOS Xcode integrated development environment (IDE) up and running. You will be guided in creating tutorial projects that will become your porting sample projects. I believe this is the best way for you to get hands-on experience while learning programming topics.

Part II of this book shows you how to plan and structure your iOS apps by creating a storyboard and breaking the app into model-view-controller (MVC) classes. The common mobile topics are followed, including creating a user interface, managing data, and enabling networking with remote services. You will then be able to create simple but meaningful iOS apps with rich UI components and be able to handle common create, read, update, delete (CRUD) operations locally and remotely.

Last, part III walks you through a case study for a complete iOS app. It recaps the topics in this book. You can also use the book's table of contents or index to help find the mobile topics you need.

A bonus chapter was added in the end reveals how to mix and match web front development with iOS SDK, the so-called hybrid apps. You may choose to bundle the web contents and HTML pages with Javascript code just like you normally do for frontend web apps. You can interface with the native iOS platform features and communicate between your JavaScript and iOS code back and forth.

When you complete this journey, you will be able to use Xcode and Swift to effectively implement simple and meaningful iOS apps.

Part **1**

Prepare Your Tools

1

Setting Up the Development Environment

It is more fun to see apps run than to read the source code, and you cannot get hands-on programming experience by just reading books. Let's get the development environment up and running first so you can use it—and learn Swift programming for iOS along the way.

There is no single integrated development environment (IDE) that can be called *the* IDE for web development. Eclipse and Eclipse-based products such as Aptana and Spket, and others such as NetBeans, IntelliJ Idea, and Visual Studio, are all popular tools for building and deploying web applications. In fact, some outstanding web developers use only a text editor to create Hypertext Markup Language (HTML), Cascading Style Sheets (CSS), or JavaScript files! In the iOS programming world, Apple purposely requires a single development environment for creating iOS apps. It makes for no jailbreakers, and all you need is the one tool: Xcode.

> **Note** Rather than attempt to provide specific examples from every web IDE, this book will instead reference analogous tasks from web development where applicable.

Xcode and the iOS SDK

Xcode is a complete tool set for building iOS apps. In other words, it is an IDE that helps you build, test, debug, and package your iOS apps. It is free, but you must have an Intel-based Mac running Mac OS X Mavericks or newer. You will use the latest Xcode, version 6, throughout this book.

Installing from the Mac App Store

Xcode is distributed via the Mac App Store, which takes care of the download and install for you. With a single click to start the download and installation of Xcode, you get the compilers, code editor, iOS software development kit (SDK), debugger, device emulators, and everything you need to create iOS apps. Figure 1-1 shows Xcode in the Mac App Store.

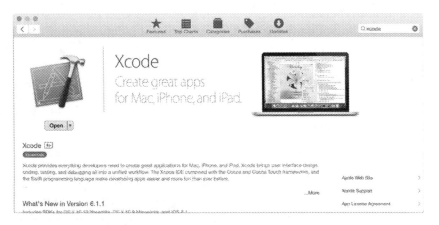

Figure 1-1. Xcode in Mac App Store

All you need to do is install the latest Xcode from the App Store. After completing the installation, launch Xcode from the Applications folder. Keep it in the Mac OS Dock so that you can launch it at any time.

The first time you launch Xcode, it immediately prompts you to install the required components (see Figure 1-2). Click Install to complete the Xcode installation.

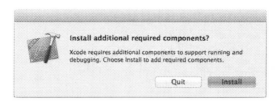

Figure 1-2. Install the required components

After the required components are installed, you should see the screen in Figure 1-3. Your iOS IDE, Xcode, is ready!

Figure 1-3. Welcome to Xcode screen

Creating an iOS Project Using the Template

WEB ANALOGY

You can create a New Web Application project in Visual Studio, create a new project in Sencha Architect (and select a framework), use the web app project templates in Eclipse web projects, and so on.

You've got the right tool; now, wouldn't you like to see some real action— like creating an iOS app and seeing it run? I'd like that, too! You want to do this to ensure your IDE is working properly as well.

Out of the box, Xcode offers the project creation templates that immediately give you a starting point that contains the minimal software artifacts for the given project types. The objective of this section is to show you how to create an iOS app as quickly as possible. Hold any programming questions so you can finish the project as fast as you can. For now, complete the following steps:

1. Launch Xcode if you haven't launched it yet.

2. Click "Create a new Xcode project" on the Welcome to Xcode screen (shown earlier in Figure 1-3). Figure 1-4 shows the prompt that asks you to choose a template for your project.

   a. In the left panel of Figure 1-4, select iOS ➤ Application.

   b. In the right panel of Figure 1-4, you may choose any of the templates. Just for fun, choose Game.

Figure 1-4. Choose a template

3. Click the Next button.

4. Figure 1-5 depicts the basic project information that requires you to fill in the following:

   a. *Product Name*: This is the app name. Name your project LessonOne.

   b. *Organization Name*: This is optional; for example, you can use your organization's name or any name you choose.

c. *Organization Identifier:* Together with the product
    name, the organization identifier should uniquely
    identify your app. A reverse domain name is
    recommended (for example, com.yourdomain.xxx).

d. *Language*, *Game Technology*, and *Devices*:
    You don't need to change these settings.

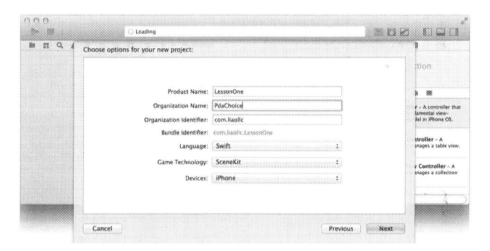

Figure 1-5. iOS project options

5. Click the Next button when done.

6. Select a folder in which to save your LessonOne
    project.

That is it! You just created an iOS project, the LessonOne project, that you
can see the in Xcode as shown in Figure 1-6.

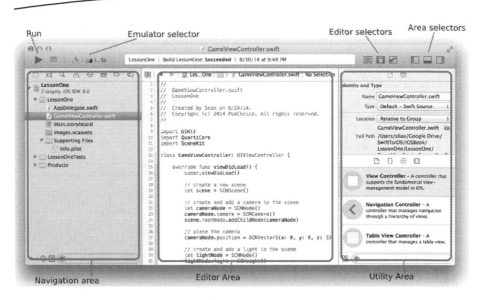

Figure 1-6. LessonOne project in Xcode Project Navigator (left panel)

The LessonOne project can be seen on the left panel, as shown in Figure 1-6; this is the Project Navigator in the navigation area. The Xcode project template creates the project folder, the application source code, and all the resources for building the LessonOne apps.

Building the Project

> ### WEB ANALOGY
>
> This is the process that bundles, minifies, and packages your app and all the referenced code that will be deployed with it.

To build and compile the Xcode project, use the Build action, which is located in the Product ➤ Build menu in Xcode (or press ⌘+B). You will get used to using the ⌘+B keyboard shortcut a lot because Xcode doesn't automatically build your code (unlike Eclipse ADT, which builds it automatically by default).

Launching the App

The LessonOne project should have no errors. You can launch the app and see it run on an iOS emulator. The emulator is an important piece of any IDE, probably even more important for mobile apps. All the iOS devices emulators are right there in Xcode, and you can launch the LessonOne project on the selected device, including the iOS emulator, by clicking the triangle button in the upper-left corner, as shown earlier in Figure 1-6.

Alternatively, you can use the ⌘+R Xcode keyboard shortcut key for the Run action to launch the app. You should see your LessonOne app running on the iPhone emulator, as shown in Figure 1-7.

Figure 1-7. LessonOne app in the emulator

Play with the app and then select other emulators from the device drop-down selector (see the pointer in Figure 1-6). A mouse-click event on an emulator is equivalent to a touch event, and three-finger movement on the trackpad is equivalent to a touch-drag on a physical iOS screen. If you don't have a particular device yet, definitely play with the emulator to get familiar with the emulated iOS devices.

> **Tip** To change to landscape or portrait orientation, press ⌘+left arrow
> or ⌘+right arrow to rotate the emulator.

The iOS emulators are robust and responsive, and they behave almost exactly like real devices. For learning Swift programming for iOS, the emulator actually is better. In this book, you are not required to run apps on a physical iOS device; for that you would need to be a registered iOS developer. You can save the $99 iOS developer membership fee until you are ready to submit your first app to the App Store or for when your app requires certain features not available in the emulator (for example, the camera or certain sensors). For your convenience, I have provided how to build and sign an app for on-device debugging in the appendix of this book. For now, if your app is launched and running on an iOS emulator, your mission is completed!

Summary

By installing Xcode 6, you immediately have a fully functional IDE ready to create iOS apps without hassle. This chapter walked you through the basic project creation tasks in Xcode 6, using an iOS project template to start your first iOS project. This chapter also showed you how to build and run your iOS app in iOS emulators. You haven't written any code yet, but your Xcode tool is working and verified. You will learn more and gain hands-on programming experience from the guided exercises in the following chapters.

Chapter 2

iOS Programming Basics

Creating mobile apps for both iOS and web deployment is fun and rewarding. With Xcode in place, you are ready to write code, build, and run iOS apps now. Objective-C had been the primary programming language for iOS apps until Swift was officially announced at the 2014 Apple Worldwide Developers Conference. If you're just starting to learn iOS programming, you should go with Swift because there is no reason to choose the old way and miss the latest and greatest features. Your next steps should be learning the fundamentals of the following:

- The Swift programming language
- The anatomy of the iOS project and the Xcode storyboard editor

The purpose of this chapter is to get you comfortable with reading the Swift code in this book. To achieve this goal, you will be creating a HelloSwift project while learning about Swift programming language highlights.

You will create another Xcode iOS project in the second part of the chapter. All iOS apps have a user interface (UI). You normally start by creating the UI using the most important Xcode tool, the storyboard editor, which draws the UI widgets and components and connects them to your code. You also will see the typical iOS project structures and components while creating this iOS app. You may not need to understand everything about the iOS framework in the beginning, but the first storyboard lesson should be "just enough" for you to get a feel for the different programming paradigm. Later, the materials in Chapters 3 and 4 continue with step-by-step instructions for common programming tasks and framework topics. Follow these mapping instructions, and the ideas will more easily stick with you as you get a broader picture of the whole app.

The Swift Language in a Nutshell

Swift is the newest programming language for creating iOS apps. I am confident that learning the Swift language won't be the highest hurdle for you; JavaScript and C# developers will pick up Swift code naturally because they are syntactically similar and follow the conventions of typical object-oriented (OO) programming languages. Just to give you a quick preview, Table 2-1 briefly compares JavaScript to Swift.

Table 2-1. Java-to-Swift Language Syntax Comparison in a Nutshell

JavaScript	Swift
`<script type="text/javascript" src="scripts/packagename/Xyz.js"> </script>`	**`import`** `framework`
`Xyz.prototype = new SomeClass();`	**`class`** `Xyz : SomeClass`
`var mProperty;`	**`var`** `mProperty : ` **`Int`**
`Xyz.prototype.constructor=Xyz // constructor`	`init()`
`var obj = new Xyz();`	`var obj : Xyz = Xyz()`
`Xyz.prototype.doWork(arg)`	**`func`** `doWork (arg: String)` **->** `Void`
`obj.doWork(arg);`	`obj.doWork(arg)`

The Table 2-1 cross-reference refers to how native JavaScript prototype-based inheritance might be used to implement classical inheritance used by Swift, Java, and C#. For those familiar with Prototype and Sencha, the extension libraries and methods for inheritance should make the transition even more straightforward. If you come from a basic JQuery programming background, the syntax of Swift will seem familiar, but the structure of your code will move from a flat list of functions to encapsulated objects and object instances with a hierarchal source structure. In this section, I will not discuss the in-depth OO theory or techniques. However, I do want to point out certain important ideas for pure-JavaScript developers.

HelloSwift with Xcode

Instead of my describing the uses and syntax rules in a formal way, you are going to create a HelloSwift Xcode project and write the code listing from Table 2-1 yourself. You will also perform the following common Xcode programming tasks: creating a class, building and running a project, and using the debugger.

Creating a Swift Command-Line Project

Let's create a command-line Swift program because it is really simple and you can focus on the Swift language without being sidetracked by other questions.

Follow these instructions to proceed:

1. Launch Xcode 6 if it is not running. You should see the Welcome to Xcode screen. Click "Create a new Xcode project." Alternatively, you can select File ➤ Project from the Xcode menu bar.

2. Choose OS X and then Application in the left column and then select the Command Line Tool template in the "Choose a template for your new project" window (see Figure 2-1).

Figure 2-1. Choosing an Xcode template

3. To finish creating the new project with the template, follow the same onscreen instructions that you used to create the LessonOne project in Chapter 1:

    a. *Product Name*: Enter **HelloSwift**.

    b. *Organization Name*: You can use anything here, such as PdaChoice.

    c. *Organization Identifier*: You can use anything here, such as com.liaollc.

    d. Language: Select Swift.

4. Click the Next button when done.

5. Select a folder in which to save your HelloSwift project.

6. The HelloSwift project appears in the Project Navigator (see Figure 2-2).

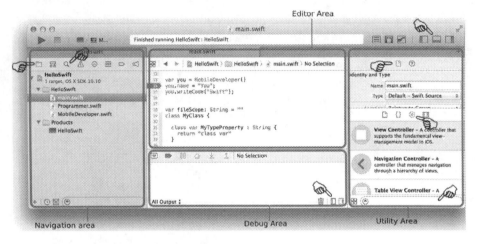

Figure 2-2. *Creating the HelloSwift project*

The command-line template creates the `main.swift` file for you. This is the entry point of the OS X command line tool program. You will be writing code in `main.swift` to demonstrate common object-oriented code.

Figure 2-2 shows that the typical Xcode workspace contains three areas from left to right and a top toolbar. Inside each area, there are subviews that you may switch to using the selector bars.

■ The Project Navigator area is on the left. Similar to many IDE, this is where you can see the whole project structure and select the file you want to edit. There are other views in this area; for example, you can enable Search view by selecting the Search icon in the selector bar.

■ The Editor area in the middle shows the selected file in its editor, in which you can edit the file, write your code, or modify project settings depending on the file selected. The Console and Variable views are inside the Debug area. Most likely you will want to show them during debugging sessions. You can hide or show them by clicking the toggle buttons on the top and bottom toolbars.

▓   The Utility area on the right contains several inspector views that allow you to edit attributes of the whole file or the item selected in the Editor area. Depending on the type of files you select, different types of inspectors will be available in the top selector bar. For example, you will have more inspectors showing in the selector bar if you are editing a screen or UI widgets. The bottom of the area is called the Libraries area. Use the selector bar to select one of the library views. You can drag and drop items from Libraries to the appropriate editor to visually modify file content. You will use the Object Library a lot to compose UIs visually.

Click any of the icons on the selector bars, or hover your mouse over the pointer in Figure 2-2, to see the hover text tips in the workspace to get yourself familiar with Xcode workspace. The subviews appear more condensed than those in most of the IDE I ever experienced, but essentially it is a tool for the same purpose: editing project files and compiling, building, debugging, and running the executables. You will use it repeatedly throughout the book.

Creating a Swift Class

A class is the fundamental building block of any classic OO programming language. A class is a software template that defines what the objects know (state) and how the objects behave (methods). JavaScript uses functions and their prototypes to accomplish the same goal.

While JavaScript web applications often make use of objects by creating and manipulating DOM elements, it is entirely possible to create a JavaScript web application without creating a single new reusable object structure. Using anonymous objects and scripts running in the global scope, referencing function libraries like JQuery, is quite common. Swift, however, requires developers to structure their code into named class types before the objects can be created.

To create a new Swift class, you can create it in the existing `main.swift` file, or you can follow the Java convention to create it in its own file as shown in the following steps:

1. Expand the newly created HelloSwift project, right-click the `HelloSwift` folder to bring up the folder context menu (see Figure 2-3), and select New File.

    a. Select iOS and then Source from the left panel and then select the Swift File template in the "Choose a template for your new file" screen.

    b. Save the file and name it `MobileDeveloper.swift`. The file should appear in your project.

Figure 2-3. Create a Swift class from the folder context menu

2.   Enter the code in Listing 2-1 in the `MobileDeveloper.`
     `swift` file to create the `MobileDeveloper` Swift class.

Note   Unlike Java, a Swift class doesn't implicitly inherit from any class.
It can be the base class on its own.

Listing 2-1. Declare MobileDeveloper Class

```
class MobileDeveloper {

}
```

3.   Create a property called `name` by declaring a variable
     inside the class (see Listing 2-2). This is called a
     stored property in Swift, where the variable type is
     inferred by the assigned value (known as *type
     inference* in Swift).

Listing 2-2. Stored Property in Swift

```
class MobileDeveloper {
    var name  = "" // var type, String, is inferred by the value
}
```

> **Note**   The semicolon (;) is optional for terminating a statement in the same line.

Creating a Swift Protocol

WEB ANALOGY

Though JavaScript has no native comparable for a Swift protocol, web developers using C# or PHP for their server-side code will find comparable examples in the use of interfaces.

In object-oriented programming (OOP), an interface or protocol is essentially a predefined set of behaviors, methods, or properties. The protocol provides no implementation of the methods themselves but rather defines the method names, parameters, and return types. Consumers of the protocol can count on objects they are consuming to properly implement the items defined in the protocol. Protocols allow objects of different types and class inheritance to provide a common, strongly typed interface, thus implementing the concept of polymorphism, one of the fundamental concepts of OOP. You may also provide multiple implementation classes for the same contract and programmatically supply the appropriate instances in the runtime.

In simpler terms, this is a great way to explicitly break dependencies between callers and callees because callers and callees can be implemented independently with clearly defined programming contracts, called *protocols* in Swift.

Create a Swift protocol called Programmer by doing the following:

1. Right-click the HelloSwift folder to create the Programmer.swift file.

2. In the Editor area, create the Programmer protocol with the method writeCode(...), as shown in Listing 2-3.

Listing 2-3. Declare the Programmer Protocol

```
protocol Programmer {
  func writeCode(arg: String) -> Void
}
```

Implementing the Protocol

To conform to the expected behavior defined in a Swift protocol, the tagged class must implement the methods defined in the protocol. To make the MobileDeveloper class implement the Programmer protocol, do the following:

1. Modify MobileDeveloper.swift and declare the MobileDeveloper class to implement the Programmer protocol, as shown in Listing 2-4.

    Listing 2-4. Conform to MobileDeveloper Protocol

    ```
    class MobileDeveloper : Programmer {
      ...
    }
    ```

Note   If the Swift class already has a superclass, list the superclass name before any protocols it adopts, followed by a comma (,)—for example:

```
class MobileDeveloper : Person, Programmer
```

---

2. Provide the writeCode(...) method implementation body, as shown in Listing 2-5.

    Listing 2-5. Method Body

    ```
    class MobileDeveloper: Programmer {
      ...
      func writeCode(arg: String) -> Void {
        println("\(self.name) wrote: Hello, \(arg)")
      }
    }
    ```

Note   \(self.name) is evaluated first inside the quoted String literal.

Using the Swift Instance

```
                          WEB ANALOGY
```

```
var you = new MobileDeveloper();
you.setName("You");
you.writeCode("Javascript");
```

You have created a Swift MobileDeveloper class and implemented the Programmer obligations in pretty much the same way you would in Java with some minor syntax differences. To use the class, it is the same as Java in principle, calling a method defined in the receiver from the sender. Modify HelloSwift/main.swift as shown in Listing 2-6.

Listing 2-6. Swift Entry main.swift

```
var you = MobileDeveloper()
you.name = "You"
you.writeCode("Java")
```

Implementing Access Control

```
                          WEB ANALOGY
```

While JavaScript doesn't have access control keywords, many JavaScript developers use closures and constructor variables to create methods and variables with private access from the object.

Here's an example:

```
function MyObject() {
    var private;
    this.getPrivate = function (arg) {
        return private;
    }
```

```
    this.setPrivate = function (val) {
        private=val;
    }
}

var test =new MyObject();
test.setVal("My private value");
console.log("Private value is "+test.getVal());
```

Encapsulation is one of the fundamental principles of OOP; in a nutshell, certain internal states or methods are meant only for internal implementations but not to be used directly by the callers. Swift provides access controllers to prevent access to the members or methods that developers decide to hide. This is achieved with access modifiers for files and with module access controls using the following keywords as the access modifiers: private, public, and internal. The internal access modifier is the default access control that is public to the whole module but not visible when the modules are imported. If you are building a reusable module that can be imported by other program, use the public access modifier to expose the API to another module. The private access modifier makes your custom classes or type or members visible only within the file scope.

To demonstrate the private access control, modify MobileDeveloper.swift as shown in Listing 2-7.

Listing 2-7. The private Access Modifier in MobileDeveloper

```
private class MobileDeveloper {
  var name   = "" // var type is infered by the value

  func writeCode(arg: String) -> Void {
    // some dummy implementation
    println("\(self.name) wrote: Hello, \(arg)")
  }

  private func doPrivateWork() {
    println(">> doPrivateWork")
  }
}

// another class in the same source file
class TestDriver {
  func testDoPrivateWork() -> Void {
    var developer = MobileDeveloper()
    developer.doPrivateWork()
  }
}
```

Since TestDriver is implemented in the same source file, the code in
TestDriver still can access the private class and its private method.
However, the MobileDeveloper class in Listing 2-6 becomes not visible
anymore from the main.swift file.

Using the Xcode Debugger

Knowing how to use the debugger when creating software can make a
big difference in your productivity. Do the following to see the common
debugging tasks in the Xcode debugger:

1. To set a breakpoint, click the line number in the
    Xcode code editor. Figure 2-4 depicts a breakpoint
    that was set in the main.swift file.

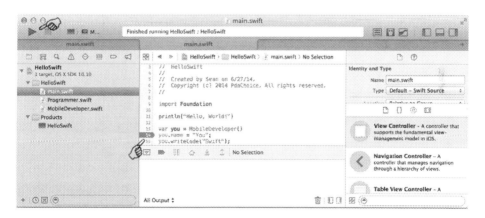

Figure 2-4. Breakpoint

> **Note**   To turn on line numbers in Xcode editors, go to the Xcode top
> menu bar and select Xcode ➤ Preferences ➤ Text Editing ➤ Show Line
> Numbers. There are other handy settings there that you may want to look
> at (for example, shortcut keys are defined under Key Binding).

2. To run the HelloSwift project, click the triangle-
    shaped Run button in the upper-left corner or press
    ⌘+R (see Figure 2-5).

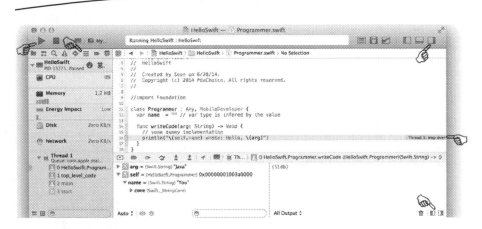

Figure 2-5. Xcode debugging

　　3.　The Swift program should start and then stop at the breakpoint as shown in Figure 2-5. While debugging, I normally toggle the following subviews on or off as needed:

　　　　a.　Hide the navigation area or switch to the Debug Navigator to view threads.

　　　　b.　Show the Debug area with the Debug toolbar and Variable and Console views.

　　　　c.　Hide the Utility area.

Stack Trace (in Debug navigator), Variables Inspector, Output Console, and the Debug toolbar (in Debug area) have a similar look and feel in most IDEs, including Xcode.

This completes your HelloSwift application exercise. As you follow along with the iOS projects in this book, you will discover more productivity tips in the Xcode IDE.

More About the Swift Language

The new Xcode environment and the Swift language have some pretty neat features, so it's worth taking a quick look at them now.

To go through this section, it is best to use the new Xcode feature called *playgrounds*. Launch Xcode and select "Get started with a playground." You can write any code snippets you want and see the result or syntax errors immediately. Figure 2-6 shows the playground; you write code in the left panel, and the right panel renders the result immediately.

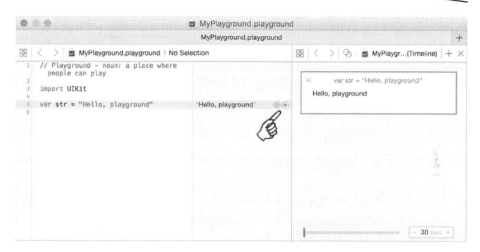

Figure 2-6. Xcode playground

JAVASCRIPT ANALOGY

Browser developer tools, JavaScript console, or JSFiddle give you immediate feedback for the Javascript code you write.

Variables and Constants

You declare a variable using the `var` keyword, and you use `let` to declare constants. Similar to JavaScript, Swift variables are global if defined not within any enclosing brackets. Listing 2-8 depicts the usage of Swift variables.

Listing 2-8. Common Variables Usages

```
var GlobalVar : String = "Global Variable"; // global scope not enclosed in
any brackets

class MyClass {
  var mProperty : String = ""; // class scope
  let mConstant : Int = 0; // constant

  func myMethod(arg : String) {
    var aVar : String = ""; // local variable in method scope
    let aConstant = 1;
  }
}
```

Type Safety and Type Inference

Unlike Swift, JavaScript is a weakly typed language. A JavaScript variable can be assigned values of any type or passed as a parameter to a function that expects a value of a completely different type or no parameters at all. JavaScript's lack of strong typing can result in code that is vulnerable to runtime errors, especially as web applications grow in size and complexity.

As a strongly typed language, Swift requires that all variables be declared with a type that they will keep through their lifetime, with the compiler flagging any mismatched types. If the type of a variable can be inferred by its value, you don't need to explicitly declare the type. Listing 2-9 is essentially the same as Listing 2-8. The Swift type inference feature encourages developers to assign initial values that reduce common errors because of variables not initialized yet.

Listing 2-9. Common Type Inference Usages

```
var GlobalVar = "Global Variable"

class MyClass {
  var mProperty = ""
  let mConstant = 0

  func myMethod(arg : String) {
    var aVar = "";
    let aConstant = 1
  }
}
```

Optional Variable

The optional variables are declared with the type and a postfixed question mark (?), called an *optional type*. This indicates the value it contains may be absent (nil, equivalent to undefined in JavaScript) for the intended type. For example, Listing 2-10 depicts the difference in Swift and JavaScript for converting a string to an integer.

Listing 2-10. Optional Type in Swift vs. Handle Exception in JavaScript

```
////// Javascript TypeError
function StringToInt(str) {

}
var intStr;
var int
```

```
function useObject(objParm) {
      try {
          objParm.badFunction()
      } catch(err) {
          console.log(err);
      }
}

var undefinedObject;
useObject(undefinedObject);

////// Swift Optional Int
var intStr = "123"
var myInt : Int? = intStr.toInt() // myInt can be nil
```

Optionals make the Swift language more type-safe and more robust by encouraging developers to understand whether the variable can be absent. Listing 2-11 demonstrates two practical Swift optional usages.

- ▓ Forced unwrapping, which uses a postfixed exclamation pointer (!)

- ▓ Optional binding, which automatically unwrap the variable in the `if` or `while` statement

Listing 2-11. Swift Optional Int

```
var intStr = "123"
var myOptionalInt : Int? = intStr.toInt() // Optional Int
if myOptionalInt != nil {
  var myInt = myOptionalInt! // Unwrap Int? to Int
  println("unwrapped Int: \(myInt)")
}

// optional binding used in if and while local scope.
if var myInt = intStr.toInt() {
  // myInt is auto unwrapped
  println("unwrapped and local scope: \(myInt)")
}
```

Implicitly Unwrapped Optionals

For the situations where a variable will always have a value after the value is set, you declare the variable as an implicitly unwrapped optional postfixed with ! instead of ?, as in `var delegate: MyDelegate!`.

Any of the optionals' usages described earlier are applicable here. You treat them as optionals, but you don't need to force unwrapping the variable (Implicitly Unwrapped Optionals). You commonly see this usage in the iOS framework for properties that are initialized somewhere else (in other words, by the caller). Particularly, iOS frameworks embed delegate properties everywhere. These delegates are declared as implicitly unwrapped optionals, but their values are typically assigned by the caller. As another example, UI widgets are normally drawn in the storyboard editor and connect to your code as IBOutlet properties. These IBOutlet properties are declared as implicitly unwrapped optionals. I just wanted to give you a quick heads up for now because you will see these usages frequently later in this book.

Tuples

WEB ANALOGY

Tuples are equivalent to JavaScript objects created by literal notation, sometimes called anonymous objects.

Here's an example:

```
var xyz  = {x: 2, y: 3, z: 0};
var total=xyz.x+xyz.y;
console.log("Total is now:"+total);
// Displays: total is now 5
```

Tuples group multiple values into a single compound value. For example, you can pass or return multiple values without creating a class or a struct (structs are also supported in Swift). Listing 2-12 shows the most common tuple usages.

Listing 2-12. Common Tuple Usages

```
var xyz  = (x: 0, y: 0, z: 0)
println("xyz \(xyz) x is: \(xyz.x)\ty is: \(xyz.y)\tz is: \(xyz.z)")

// or decompose tuples
var xy : (Int, Int) = (1, 1) // or simply var xy = (1, 1)
var (a, b) = xy
println("xy \(xy) x is: \(a)\ty is: \(b)")

func httpResponse() -> (rc: Int, status: String) {
  return (200, "OK")
}

var resp = httpResponse()
println("resp is: \(resp.rc)\t\(resp.status)")
```

Collections

```
                          JAVASCRIPT ANALOGY
```

JavaScript arrays are used as collections, having case-sensitive string names as the unique index.

Here's a JavaScript example:

```
var colors = ['red','green','blue'];
var colorDictionary = {};
colorDictionary.red = colors[0];
```

Array and Dictionary are the two Swift collections. Listing 2-13 shows the common usages, which include the following:

- Initialization
- Accessing and modifying elements using subscript syntax
- Common collection APIs

Listing 2-13. Common Array and Dictionary Usages

```
// collections
var emptyArray = Array<String>() // or [String]()
var emptyDict = Dictionary<Int, String>() // [Int: String]()
var colors = ["red", "green", "blue"]
var colorDictionary = ["r" : "red", "g" : "green", "b" : "blue"]
colors.append("alpha") // or: colors += "alpha"
colorDictionary["a"] = colors[3]
colors.insert("pink", atIndex: 2)
colors.removeAtIndex(2)
println(colors.isEmpty ? "empty" : "\(colors.count)")
```

The constant Dictionary or Array is immutable, meaning it is not allowed to add or remove elements or modify existing items. On the other hand, the variable Dictionary or Array is mutable. JavaScript has no concept of constants or access modifiers.

Control Flow

Similar to JavaScript, in Swift you use `if` and `switch` to make conditionals and use `for-in`, `for`, `while`, and `do-while` to make loops. Parentheses around the condition or loop variable are optional. Braces around the body are required. Listing 2-14 demonstrates the following common control flow usages:

- ▓ for-loop

- ▓ for-in

- ▓ while-loop

Listing 2-14. Control Flows

```
for (var idx = 0; idx < 10; idx++) { // optional parenthesis
  println("for-loop: \(idx)")
}

for item in [1,2,3,4,5] { // or for item in 1...5
  println("for-in: \(item)")
}

for c in "HelloSwift" { // loop thru characters
  print(c)
}

for (key, value) in colorDictionary {
  println("for-in dictionary:\(key) - \(value)")
}

// while-loop, or do-while that run at least once
var idx = 0
while idx < colors.count {
  println("while-loop:  \(colors[idx])")
  idx++
}
```

Switch

In Swift, the switch cases can be any types in addition to `int` primitive data. Listing 2-15 shows the following improved control flow `switch` usages in Swift:

- ▓ Combined cases and always break implicitly

- ▓ Cases with ranges

- ▓ Cases with tuples

Listing 2-15. Improved Switch

```
var condition = "red"
switch condition {
case "red", "green", "blue": // combined cases
  println("\(condition) is a prime color")
  // always break implicitly (no follow thru)
case "RED", "GREEN", "BLUE":
  println("\(condition) is a prime color in uppercase")
default: // not optional anymore
  println("\(condition) is not prime color")
}

var range = 9 // by range
switch range {
case 0:
  println("zero")
case 0...9:
  println("one-digit number")
case 10...99:
  println("two-digit number")
case 10...999: // first hit first
  println("three-digit number")
default:
  println("four or more digits")
}

var coord = (0, 1)
switch coord { // by tuples
case (0...Int.max, 0...Int.max):
  println("1st quad")
case (Int.min...0, 0...Int.max):
  println("2nd quad")
case (Int.min...0, Int.min...0):
  println("3rd quad")
case (0...Int.max, Int.min...0):
  println("4th quad")
default:
  println("on axis")
}
```

A switch can bind the matched value within its local scope. You can specify a where clause to test the condition, too. Listing 2-16 demonstrates both value bindings.

Listing 2-16. Temporary Value Binding and Using the where Clause

```
var rect = (10, 10)
switch rect {
case let (w, h) where w == h:
  println("\((w, h)) is a square")
default:
  println("rectangle but not square")
}
```

Enumerations

You use an enum to define a common type for a group of named and related constant values. JavaScript has no analogous concept, often leaving developers passing numeric values to functions with code comments to explain the meaning of each numeric value. After the enumeration is defined, you use it just as a Swift type that is type-safe. Listing 2-17 shows the following common enum usages:

- Enum with or without raw values

- Enum associated with values

Listing 2-17. Common Enum Usages

```
enum DayOfWeek { // raw value is optional
  case SUNDAY, MONDAY, TUESDAY, WEDNESDAY,
  THURSDAY, FRIDAY, SATURDAY
}

var aDay = DayOfWeek.SUNDAY
switch aDay {
case DayOfWeek.SATURDAY, DayOfWeek.SUNDAY:
  println("\(aDay) is weekend")
default:
  println("\(aDay) is weekday")
}

enum DayOfWeek2 :  String { // assign raw value
  case SUNDAY = "Sun", MONDAY = "Mon", TUESDAY = "Tue",
  WEDNESDAY = "Wed", THURSDAY = "Thu", FRIDAY = "Fri", SATURDAY = "Sat"
}

var aDay2 = DayOfWeek2.SUNDAY
switch aDay2 {
case DayOfWeek2.SATURDAY, DayOfWeek2.SUNDAY:
  println("\(aDay2.rawValue) is weekend")
```

```
default:
  println("\(aDay2.rawValue) is weekday")
}

// associated values
enum Color {
  case RGB(Int, Int, Int)
  case HSB(Float, Float, Float)
}

var aColor = Color.RGB(255, 0, 0)
switch aColor {
case var Color.RGB(r, g, b):
  println("R: \(r) G: \(g) B: \(b) ")
default:
  println("")
}
```

Functions

Swift functions are declared with the func keyword. Unlike JavaScript functions, which do not declare a return type, the parameter and return types must be declared after the parameter names and function signature. Here are the typical Swift function usages you most likely will encounter (see Listing 2-18):

- *Tuples*: You can return multiple values without creating a struct or class (see Listing 2-11).

- *External parameter names*: You should treat external parameter names as part of the function signature. All of the iOS Objective-C SDK APIs are ported to Swift with external parameter names.

- *Default parameter values*: Not only does this feature provide a default value, but it also makes method overloading easier in many situations, as opposed to method chaining.

- *Variadic parameters*: This is convenient to specify functions with variable number of function parameters without using Array type.

- *Function parameters*: These are constant by default.

- *Swift functions*: These are of a reference type. Just as you can with a class type, you can pass functions as function parameters or return them as function return types. In practice, you would use closure expressions more frequently.

- *Closure expression*: This is one of the three types of closure defined in Swift. It is an unnamed self-contained block of code that can be passed as a function parameter.

> **Note**   The second type of closure is the global function mentioned right here, which is actually a special case of closure. The third type of closure is called a *nested function* declared inside a function, which is not used in this book.

Listing 2-18. Function Usages

```
func doWork(parm : String) -> String { // simple form
   return "TODO: " + parm
}
println(doWork("Swift"))

// External parameter names is part of the func signature
func doWork2(name parm : String) -> String {
// arg = arg.uppercaseString; // error: constant parm
   return "TODO: " + parm
}
println(doWork2(name: "Swift"))

// use # to indicate same name for internal and external
func doWork3(#name: String) -> String {
   return "TODO: " + name
}
println(doWork3(name: "Swift"))

// With default parm value, it also implies #, same external name
func doWork4(name: String = "Swift") -> String {
   return "TODO: " + name
}
println(doWork4()) // default parm value
```

```
// parm is constant by default unless declaring it with var
func doWork5(var name: String = "Swift") -> String {
  name = name.uppercaseString;
  return "TODO: " + name;
}

// variadic parms
func sumNumbers(parms : Int...) -> Int {
  var sum = 0
  for number in parms {
    sum += number
  }
  return sum
}
println(sumNumbers(2,5,8))

// func is a type, can be used for parm or return type.
func separateByAnd(p1: String, p2: String) -> String {
  return p1 + " and " + p2
}
func printTwoString(p1: String, p2: String, format: (String, String)
->String) {
  println(format(p1, p2))
}
printTwoString("Horse", "Carrot", separateByAnd)

// closure expression is unnamed func
printTwoString("Horse", "Carrot",
  {(p1: String, p2: String) -> String in
    return p1 + " and " + p2
  })
printTwoString("Horse", "Carrot",
  {p1, p2 in // type inferences
    return p1 + " and " + p2
  })
printTwoString("Horse", "Carrot",
  { // Inference and shorthanded parm names, $0, $1 ...
    return $0 + " and " + $1
  })
```

You may get by with not using most of the shorthand options at first, but for iOS programming, you definitely will need to get used to the external parameter names because they are used heavily in iOS frameworks.

Class

Like other classic OO languages, Swift uses classes to define the shared functionality and properties of a given type. Though many web developers may be unfamiliar with the creation of classes using prototype inheritance in JavaScript, almost every web developer has made use of the JavaScript classes that define the support for DOM manipulation. The simplest Swift class form can be depicted as shown in Listing 2-19.

Listing 2-19. Simple Swift Class

```
class SimpleClass {
  var mProperty : Int = 0
  var mConstant : String = "MyKey"
  func myMethod(name: String) -> Void { println(name)}
}
```

Property

Listing 2-20 demonstrates the following Swift property usages:

- *Stored property*: Analogous to normal JavaScript object property.

- *Computed property*: For derived values, executes code, but referenced as a property.

- *Property observer*: Optional coding block that responds to changes in a property value.

- *Type property*: A property with scope defined at the class level, rather than at the instance level. Stored type properties are not supported in the Swift class type yet. Since struct type property is now supported, you may choose to define an inner struct for porting Java static variables as a workaround for now.

Listing 2-20. Swift Class Property

```
class MyClass {
  var width = 10, height = 10 // stored properties

  // computed properties, can have set as well
  var size : Int {
    get {
      return width * height
    }
  }
```

```
var size2 : Int { // readonly, shorthanded
  return width * height
}

// property observer
var depth : Int = 10 {
  willSet {
    println("depth (\(depth)) will be set to \(newValue)")
  }
  didSet {
    println("depth (\(depth)) was set from \(oldValue)")
  }
}

// Swift class Type property,
class var MyComputedTypeProperty : String {
  return "Only computed Type property is supported in class type for now"
}

// use struct stored Type property as a workaround
struct MyStatic {
  static let MyConst = "final static in Java"
  static var MyVar: String?
}
}

println(MyClass.MyStatic.MyConst)
MyClass.MyStatic.MyVar = "class var in Java"
println(MyClass.MyStatic.MyVar)
```

Method

Methods are functions defined inside a type context (in other words, a class). They are still functions as described previously (see Listing 2-17). You can define instance methods, which are called on an instance of a class, or type methods, which are called on the class itself. Listing 2-21 shows the following typical method usages:

- Method declarations enforce external names implicitly, except for the first parameter. This is different from the global function (see the "Functions" section). All iOS Objective-C methods are ported to Swift using this convention.

- Use class func to declare class type methods, or use static func to declare type methods in struct or enum types.

Listing 2-21. Common Method Usages

```
class MyClass {

///////// methods copied from Listing 2-17 //////////
  func doWork(parm : String) -> String {
    return "Do something with: " + parm
  }

  // default parm value, always imply externl parm name
  func doWork2(name: String = "Swift") -> String {
    return "Do something with: " + name
  }

  // func is a type, can be used for parm or return type.
  func separateByAnd(p1: String, p2: String) -> String {
    return p1 + " and " + p2
  }

  func printTwoString(p1:String, p2:String, format:(String, String)->String)
{
    println(format(p1, p2))
  }

  // Type methods, methods which can be called on the Class
  class func DoWork(parm : String) -> String {
    return "Do something with: " + parm
  }
}

var c = MyClass()
println(c.doWork("Swift"))
println(c.doWork2()) // default parm value
println(c.doWork2(name: "Swift")) // external name enforced

// closure is unnamed func
c.printTwoString("Horse", p2: "Carrot", format: c.separateByAnd)
// Inference and shorthanded parm names apply to method, too.
c.printTwoString("Apple", p2: "Orange", format: {
  return $0 + " and " + $1
  })

MyClass.DoWork("Swift Type method")
```

Reference Type vs. Value Types

Just as in JavaScript, reference types are passed by reference (the reference to the instance is copied to another variable), and values types are passed by copy (the whole value type instance is copied to another memory space). However, you do need to pay attention to certain differences.

- Custom classes are reference types. Primitives, structs, and enums are value types. This is similar to JavaScript, where objects and functions are passed by reference and primitives are passed by value.

- Unlike JavaScript, arrays are value types (they are not classes in Swift). This is nice but may surprise you in the beginning.

- Since `Dictionary` and `Array` are value types, they are copied during assignment. The contained items are also deep-copied if they are value types.

- You will encounter the Swift `NSString`, `NSArray`, and `NSDictionary` because they are directly ported from counterpart Objective-C framework classes. They are all implemented as classes and are thus reference types.

iOS Project Anatomy

Most GUI apps are composed of more than programming source code; for example, a typical iOS project contains Swift or Objective-C source code, libraries, storyboard files, images or multimedia noncode application resources, an application-information property `Info.plist` file, and so forth. Xcode compiles and builds the whole project and bundles all the artifacts required for an app into an archive file with an `.app` file extension and signs the `.app` file with the appropriate signing certificate.

Let's create a simple `HelloMobile` Xcode project so that you can visualize these software artifacts in a typical iOS project.

- It has only one screen.

- On this screen, it has an `EditText` to take user input. When the **Hello** button is pressed, it shows a greeting in a `TextView`.

To create the HelloMobile iOS app, start Xcode and proceed with the following steps:

1. Select "Create a new Xcode project" on the Welcome to Xcode launch screen. Or, you can select File ➤ New ➤ Project from Xcode's top menu bar.

2. Select iOS Application and then choose Single View Application as the project template (see Figure 2-7).

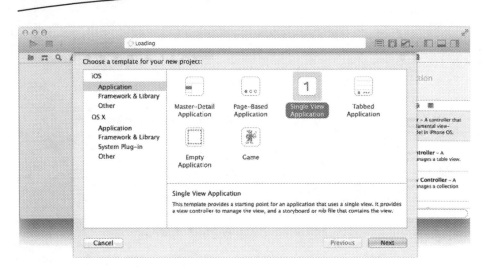

Figure 2-7. Single View Application template

3. Complete the following fields to finish creating the new project:

    a. *Product Name*: Enter **HelloMobile**.

    b. *Organization Name*: Use something like PdaChoice.

    c. *Organization Identifier*: Use something like com.liaollc.

    d. *Language*: Select Swift.

4. Click the Next button when done.

5. Select a folder to save your HelloMobile project.

The bare-bones HelloMobile iOS project is created, and it now appears in the Xcode Project Navigator area (see Figure 2-8).

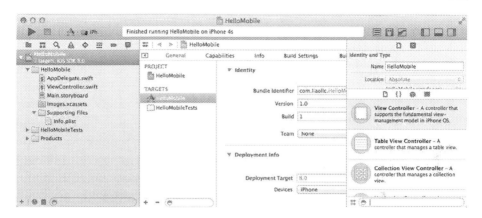

Figure 2-8. HelloMobile project

It is immediately runnable. Let's examine the typical iOS software artifacts in an Xcode project, which comprise the iOS app.

- Swift classes in .swift files. There are two classes.

    a. AppDelegate.swift: Each iOS app must have one AppDelegate class. This is the entry point of the iOS program. You don't need to modify this file if your program doesn't need to track the global application state.

    b. ViewController.swift: There is a ViewController class paired with the content view. The intended purpose is the content view controller for the content view.

- Main.storyboard file with .storyboard file extension.

    a. You commonly create one storyboard scene per content view and use only one storyboard file for all content views so you can visually implement the linkages among them.

    b. Images.xcassets. This is where you put your image assets, in what is called the *assets catalog*. Developers should provide different assets for each device configuration. This is done for the same purpose as providing alternative resources in Android.

    c. PNG and JPEG image formats are both supported as of this writing. Using the assets catalog is not a must. You may drop any resource files into the Xcode project. (You may want to create a folder to organize them yourself).

- ▓ `Info.plist` file. This file describes how the app is configured and the required capabilities the system needs to know.

    a. You may glance through this file to get a feel for the configurations and settings that Xcode needs to know about the app. Xcode initially creates it in XML format, which you can edit directly.

- ▓ Like most web development projects, you can organize your project structure in any way you want. Many web developers follow a strict naming convention pattern for the storage of their CSS files, images, and so on, and Swift will allow you to do the same. Swift currently has no concept of namespaces. All classes in Swift are scoped by the module they are defined in (that is, `NSLog` Swift scopes as `Foundation.NSLog`). I normally manually organize my Swift classes in folders structured by functionality and create a `res` folder to organize any resources files, including the `Images.xcassets`.

    a. In Xcode, the folder can be an actual folder in light blue (for example, the `Images.xcassets` folder).

    b. Folders in Xcode can also be just a tag, called a *group*, that is yellow (for example, `HelloMobile`, `Supporting Files`, and so on). Their actual location could be in any of the physical subfolders, but you should not care.

- ▓ Xcode 6 automatically creates a unit test target for your primary project. It contains a `TestCase` class skeleton in which you can write your unit test code. Although you will not use this feature in this book, it is actually useful.

- ▓ Project Settings and Target Settings instruct Xcode how to compile and build the projects. To show the Project Settings, select the top-level application name in the Xcode Project Navigator area. The Project Settings editor shows in the Editor area. For this simple project, you don't need to modify anything. But you should glance through the editor to get a quick idea of what Xcode requires to compile and build the executable.

The iOS app is not completed yet, but it has everything a typical iOS app should have.

Xcode Storyboard

WEB ANALOGY

There is no storyboard-like feature in most web dev environments. Views are normally either built one at a time in a quasi-WYSIWIG markup editor (Visual Studio, Eclipse, and so on) or, more often than not, built in a text editor for use with libraries such as Handlebars or Knockout. Even web developers familiar with Sencha Architect will find the storyboard designer's presentation of application flow to be tremendously powerful and intuitive by comparison.

Use the Xcode storyboarding feature to visually compose the UI for your app. As its name implies, not only does it create individual screens and UI widgets, but it also lets you compose the whole app as one storyboard. Since iOS apps are all GUI apps, this tool will greatly determine your productivity in creating iOS apps through the following actions:

- Drag and drop a View Controller from the Object Library to create a content view, called a *storyboard scene*.

- Drag and drop UI widgets from the Object Library onto the storyboard scene (content view) and position each widget appropriately.

- Implement Auto Layout to make the UI widgets and content view flexible and adaptive for various screen sizes, similar to the Android relative layout manager.

- Implement specific content views for specific size classes of different devices.

- Link the UI widgets to the properties of the view controller via outlets and write code to respond to UI widget events.

- You can even draw the view controller transitions all within the storyboard editor.

There are other subviews in the Utility area that you can select from the top selector toolbar. All of them are important; you should take a moment to get familiar with them.

- *File Inspector*: This shows you the actual file identity and document type options in Xcode.

- *Quick Help Inspector*: This shows you the reference doc.

■ *Identity Inspector*: This shows you the Swift class from SDK or your custom class that is associated with the item in the storyboard.

■ *Attributes Inspector*: This is your primary interest now. You will see different attributes for different widgets.

■ *Size Inspector*: This shows you the rectangular area in which the widget is located.

■ *Connections Inspector*: This lets you draw the connection to the view controller. I will discuss this later in the book (see "Interact with Content View" in Chapter 3).

Now is the time for you to get familiar with the Xcode storyboarding feature. The iOS HelloMobile project doesn't look like the complete app yet; it has only one screen in the Main.storyboard file, which is empty. You will need to add three UI widgets: EditText, TextView, and a hello Button.

First you will implement the user interface of the HelloMobile iOS app. Xcode storyboards provide everything you need for this mission.

Object Library and Attributes Inspector

WEB ANALOGY

Many web developers find themselves building their markup and code in a tool of their choosing, running the application in a browser with the developer tools open, and inspecting and manipulating the attributes of their layout directly from the browser.

You need to add three UI widgets to the content view using the following steps:

1. Select the Main.storyboard file in the Project Navigator. Figure 2-10 depicts the storyboard editor in the Editor area. Currently, there is only one screen, known as a storyboard scene.

2. Select the Object Library from the Library selector bar in the Utility area. This is where you can find the UI widgets and elements to compose the storyboard.

3. Optionally, to make more room for your storyboard editor, you may hide the navigation and Debug areas by selecting the toggle buttons, as indicated in Figure 2-9.

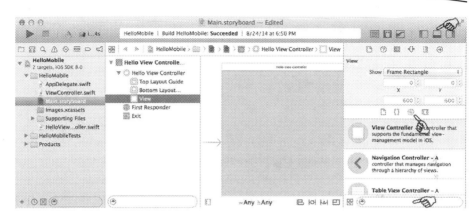

Figure 2-9. Select UI components from the Object Library

4. I will talk about size class, an important new iOS 8 feature, in Chapter 3. For now, disable it by unchecking Use Size Classes in the File Inspector of the Utility area, as shown in Figure 2-10. This will give you a better WYSIWYG storyboard editor.

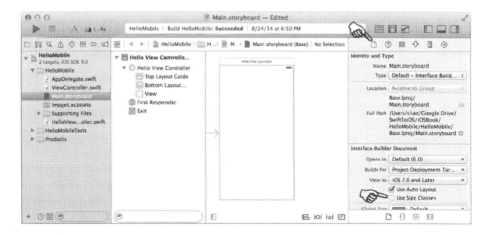

Figure 2-10. Disable Use Size Classes in File Inspector

5. To add the UI widget to storyboard scene, find the desired UI widget from the Object Library and drag it to the existing view in the storyboard scene. Both Android and iOS screens must have one root view, and any view element should be added to a parent view. This forms the parent-child view hierarchy.

a. You must select the parent view (see the pointer in Figure 2-11) first so you can drop the TextField element onto it.

b. You may browse and select the UI widgets from Object Library. The list is long, so the search bar on the bottom is useful for finding the right widget. Type the name of the iOS widget, as shown in Figure 2-10, or just type in your best guess for as many characters as needed.

Tip   The iOS widgets you need are called UITextField, UILabel, and UIButton.

---

c. To position the newly added TextField, drag it to where you want it to be. Xcode gives you guide lines to show you when the widgets are at certain positions of the common interests, such as in the center, or aligned to any other widgets (see Figure 2-11).

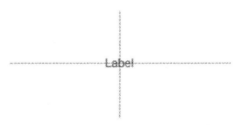

Figure 2-11. Guide lines

d. Figure 2-12 shows the three simple UI widgets added to the storyboard scene.

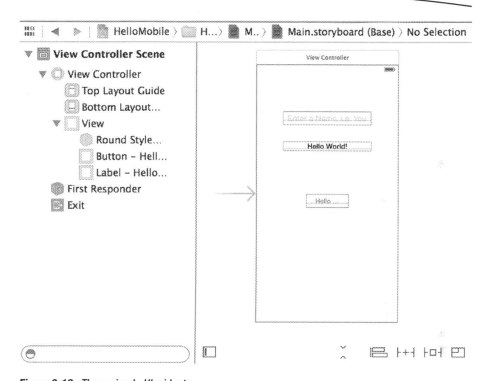

Figure 2-12. *Three simple UI widgets*

6. The attributes of UI widgets in Swift control the look,
    feel, and behavior of the widgets, and you can change
    them visually. You can find and modify these attributes
    in the Attributes Inspector located in the Utility area.
    Set the attributes of the TextField like this:

    a. Set the font size to System 24.

    b. For the placeholder, enter **Enter a Name,
        e.g., You**.

    c. Set the alignment to center.

    d. TextField has a handful of attributes. Glance
        through them and you should have no problem
        relating them to the counterpart attributes you
        normally use in an HTML element.

    e. Switch to the Size Inspector view and change
        the width to 200. You will need to drag the
        TextField to reposition it to center horizontally.

7.   To make the Label widget like the Android counterpart TextView, modify the following attributes:

    a.   For Text, enter something like **Hello World!**.

    b.   Set Font to something like System 20 or Headline.

    c.   Set Alignment to center.

    d.   Set Lines to 1.

    e.   Switch to the Size Inspector and change the width to 200. You will need to drag the label to reposition it to center horizontally.

8.   To make the Button widget like the Android counterpart, modify the following attributes:

    a.   Text: **Hello World!**

    b.   Title: **Hello ...**

9.   To preview your storyboard in Xcode, click the Assistant Editor button on the toolbar and select Preview in the Assistant Editor, as shown in Figure 2-13.

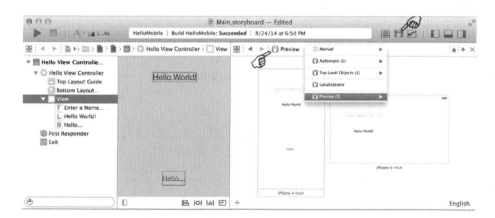

Figure 2-13. Three simple widgets added to the storyboard

The look and feel in portrait mode is close enough for our purposes, in other words, using a storyboard to visually compose the content view without writing a single line of code. The iOS HelloMobile is not completed yet. The Hello button doesn't read "Hello...," and the landscape mode is not acceptable yet. Both are important topics and have their own sections in Chapter 3.

In this exercise, I just wanted to give you a quick look at the Xcode storyboard editor. The Xcode workspace could be a little overwhelming if you are not used to using any IDE. Spend a moment to get familiar with the Xcode workspace, including the storyboard editor, the Utility area, the selector toolbar, and so forth. Xcode storyboarding is an important tool that will greatly influence your productivity when creating iOS apps.

Summary

On the surface, you learned about a lot of things in this chapter. I started with a discussion of Swift–JavaScript language comparisons to show their similarities, and then I went over Swift language topics to highlight the new language features. However, the rest of the book will focus on iOS programming instead of the Swift language. The code will address readability as opposed to being concise using shorthanded notations or Swift tricks. You surely won't have a problem reading all the Swift code in the rest of the book. Sooner or later, though, you will need the reference document to the Swift programming language, which is available free in iTunes (`https://itunes.apple.com/us/book/swift-programming-language/id881256329`).

You created a HelloMobile iOS project using Xcode to visualize a typical iOS application structure. You also got your first taste of the Xcode storyboard, which is important and which you will use for every iOS app, including all the sample projects in this book, so plan on revisiting the storyboard repeatedly.

Part 2

A Roadmap for Porting

Chapter 3

Structure Your App

To implement your software, you make design decisions based on how you'd like to structure your app in terms of organizing your code. To decide your iOS app structure up front, the top-down approach and model-view-controller (MVC) design pattern are recommended and actually embedded in the iOS software development kit (SDK) and tools. MVC may not be enforced in most of the popular web development platforms, but the vocabularies should be familiar to both front-end and back-end web developers. The techniques may vary, but the principle is the same: structure your app into three software layers consisting of the model, view, and controller.

In the iOS programming paradigm, you are encouraged to take the so-called top-down approach for creating your mobile apps, where you design the application workflow prior to detailing each individual screen. Xcode will guide you to turn on your top-down programming thinking hat.

I will discuss MVC first, followed by how to create the iOS storyboard in Xcode. With the guided screen navigation patterns, your iOS storyboard naturally breaks your iOS apps into MVC components to form the skeleton of the iOS mobile app.

Model-View-Controller

MVC breaks the graphical user interface (GUI) app into three layers. The iOS MVC design pattern specifies that a GUI application consists of a data model, a presentation view, and controller layers, as shown in Figure 3-1.

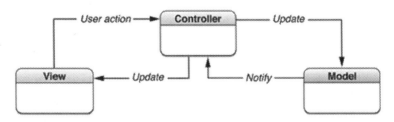

Figure 3-1. The iOS MVC design pattern

In the iOS SDK, you explicitly use the MVC vocabularies of *Content View* and *Content View Controller*. You naturally break down your iOS app into MVC classes, starting with creating a storyboard prototype using the Xcode storyboard editor.

Unless your app has only one screen, you need to decide how to implement navigation and screen transitions among multiple view controllers. You need an optional MVC participant: a Container View Controller to coordinate the view controllers. In iOS, the SDK provides several Container View Controllers for screen navigation purposes; you simply choose the appropriate Container View Controller class and let the iOS framework facilitate the tasks for you.

I'll start with the Content View and Content View Controller and then talk about the Container View Controller.

Content View

WEB ANALOGY

The Content View is equivalent to the web presentation layer. It could be a static HTML page, server-side template, or client-side template. The technique may be different, but the principle is the same: you create a presentation layer that is not tightly coupled to the data.

A Content View provides a visible area so that users can interact with the app. The Content View defines how to render itself with content and can interact with user actions. To create Content Views in iOS, use an Xcode storyboard.

When it comes down to implementing a Content View, you face the same issue you normally encounter when implementing a web page: how to make the page rendering adaptive to screen size. This is actually a hot topic in web development as well. Recall that in the iOS HelloMobile app, you drew the UI widgets in the storyboard scene by dragging and dropping the widgets to draw them on the parent view. However, this iOS Content View is not adaptive to other device types and screen orientations yet. You can easily observe the landscape problem in the Assistant Editor previews (for example, see Figure 2-14 in Chapter 2). Creating adaptive Content Views for various screen sizes is a common task in many platforms. In iOS, you essentially use iOS platform features for the same purposes.

- *Auto Layout*: This works best with responsive user experience (UX) designs that are agnostic/adaptive to screen sizes.

- *Size classes*: These provide ultimate flexibility for customizing the screens for different screen sizes.

Auto Layout

You use iOS Auto Layout to position each UI widget by aligning or spacing it relative to other widgets, that is, siblings or the parent view.

The three widgets in the current iOS HelloMobile project are not positioned properly in landscape mode (see Figure 2-14 in Chapter 2). Here you'll use iOS Auto Layout to fix this while learning its uses.

While extremely powerful, some Xcode editors and operations are collapsed in the menus and can be difficult to find for a beginner. Figure 3-2 depicts some quick tips.

- If you cannot find an editor or navigator, look in the View menu in Xcode's top menu bar.

- Auto Layout operations are grouped in the Editor menu in the Xcode top menu bar.

- There are four small buttons on the bottom toolbar of the storyboard editor. They offer quick Auto Layout operations and give you some visual hints of what they are.

- Assistant Editor is an important frequent used feature, that you will use next.

- The view selector in the Utility area allows you to switch between several inspectors. You will use inspectors a lot in the next chapter, too.

Figure 3-2. Storyboard Auto Layout operations in Xcode

Continue working on the HelloMobile project. Do the following:

1. The storyboard preview in Assistant Editor is useful for immediately seeing any changes for the selected storyboard scene.

    a. Select the `main.storyboard` file and open the Assistant Editor (see the right pointer in Figure 3-3).

    b. Select the **Preview** option from the Assistant menu selector that is default to "Automatic" (see the left pointer in Figure 3-3).

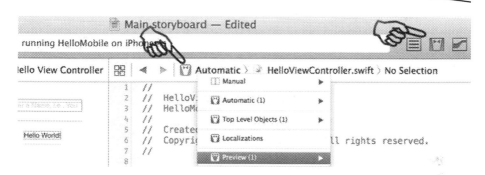

Figure 3-3. Two steps to reach the Xcode storyboard preview

2. Center the TextField horizontally in the container to create an x-alignment constraint, as shown in Figure 3-4.

   a. Select the TextField in the storyboard editor.

   b. In the Xcode top menu bar, select Editor ➤ Align ➤ Horizontal Center in Container.

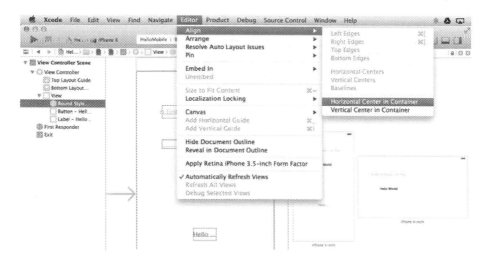

Figure 3-4. Using Horizontal Center in Container on the TextField in the Auto Layout editor

3.   Use Vertical Center in Container to create a
y-alignment constraint (see Figure 3-5).

    a.   From the Xcode top menu bar, select Editor ➤ Align ➤
Vertical Center in Container.

    b.   In the Attributes Inspector in the Utility area, to
position the TextField at the one-sixth of the view
height instead of half, you can apply a multiplier of 3.

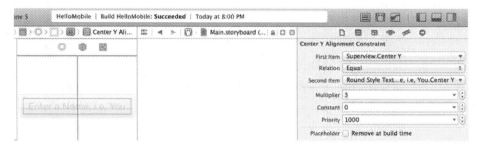

Figure 3-5. *Creating a y-alignment constraint using a multiplier*

Note   Use Multiplier or Constant to create an offset for the second
item position:

(first item position) == (second item) ∗ multiplier + constant

4.   Select Resolve Auto Layout Issues ➤ Update
Frames, as shown in Figure 3-6.

Figure 3-6. Using Update Frames to reposition the UI widgets based on constraints

5. Select the Hello World! label and click the Pin button to add multiple constraints for appropriate spacing and widgets height, as shown in Figure 3-7.

    a. Pin the Top space to the nearest widget, the TextField, with 48.5 pixels.

    b. Pin both the Leading and Trailing spaces to the nearest widget, the parent view of the label, with 60 pixels.

    c. Pin the label's Height to be 21 pixels.

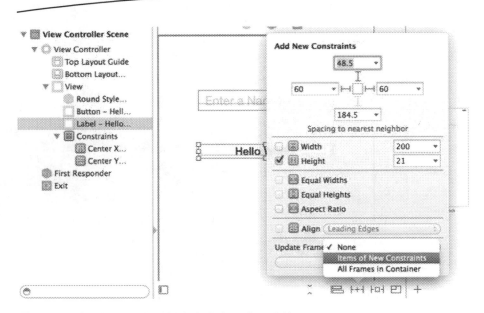

Figure 3-7. Spacing Hello World! label relative to its neighbors

> **Note**   The combined constraints need to make sense without ambiguity. You can set a priority for each individual constraint. However, if you start using priorities to resolve conflicts, you might want to think about using fewer constraints.

6.   Select the Hello World... button. You can align it similar to the TextField.

   a.   Use Horizontal Center in Container to create an x-alignment constraint.

   b.   Use Vertical Center in Container to create a y-alignment constraint with a multiplier of 0.75.

Using Auto Layout with responsive UX designs immediately provides the proper landscape layout. Figure 3-8 shows the previews in both landscape and portrait modes for iPhone 4-inch and 3.5-inch modes. Click the + icon (see the pointer in Figure 3-8) to add multiple previews for different devices.

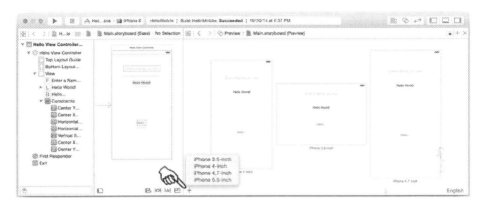

Figure 3-8. Auto Layout with responsive UX design

Size Classes

While Auto Layout provides an effective way to implement responsive UX for various screen sizes, it may not utilize the valuable mobile-screen real estate in the most efficient way. For example, it is fairly common to lay out landscape view differently from portrait because of the different aspect ratios to have tablet-specific UX design, and so forth.

Prior to iOS 8, you generally implemented two storyboards, one for iPhone and one for iPad. Beginning with iOS 8, size classes were introduced to solve this common programming issue by using the abstract presentations of device sizes in terms of horizontal widths and vertical heights. The current iOS devices can be classified as shown in Table 3-1.

Table 3-1. iOS Device Size Classes

Size Classes	Compact Width	Regular Width
	• iPhone: portrait width	• iPad: portrait width
	• iPhone: landscape width	• iPad: landscape width
Compact Height:		
• **iPhone: landscape height**	iPhone in landscape	Customized view controller
Regular Height:		
• **iPad: portrait height**	iPhone in portrait	iPad in portrait
• **iPad: landscape height**		iPad in landscape
• **iPhone: portrait height**		

You can provide the entire implementation for all size classes all in one storyboard!

Recall the iOS HelloMobile app—it works only in iPhone portrait mode (see Figure 2-14 in Chapter 2), and it disables size classes. In the following steps, you will enable size classes to see how to use them:

1. As shown in Figure 3-9, select Use Size Classes (bottom pointer) in the File Inspector (accessed as shown by the top two pointers).

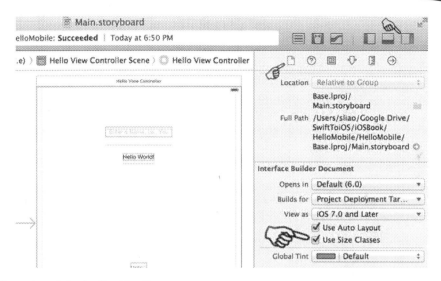

Figure 3-9. Selecting Use Size Classes

2. Use the Assistant Editor to preview the iPhone and
    iPad screens. Size classes can be overwhelming in
    the beginning, but I have found the previews helpful
    (see Figure 3-10).

    a. The scenes are converted to the most adaptive size
        class: (wAny hAny). The Auto Layout constraints are
        also preserved in this size class. You immediately get
        the iPad scene working as expected.

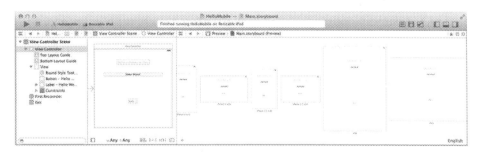

Figure 3-10. Size classes preview

3. Click the size class control to select the size class (see Figure 3-11).

   a. Hover your mouse to see the highlight and title changes. Comparing this with Table 3-1, you can select the Any row or column that targets the wider size classes. The default is Any Width | Any Height, which is applied to all the size classes to start with.

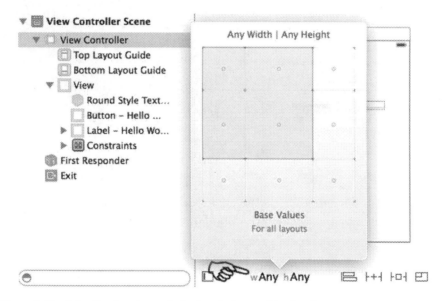

Figure 3-11. Using the size class selector to select a specific size class

4. To provide a specific layout for an iPhone landscape scene, select the Compact Width | Compact Height, as shown in Figure 3-12.

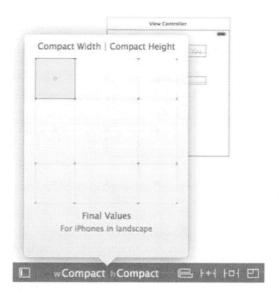

Figure 3-12. Compact Width / Compact Height for iPhones in landscape

5. To demonstrate the powerful size class feature, start fresh for the compact-compact size class. From the top menu bar, select Editor ➤ Resolve Auto Layout Issues ➤ Clear Constraints in View Controller. This clears the Auto Layout constraints only in the selected size class; you can see the constraints still there, but they are grayed out.

6. Drag the widgets to reposition them to get a quick idea—you don't need to be precise (see Figure 3-13).

    a. Since you are providing a custom layout explicitly for iPhones in landscape, you can draw the positions precisely and let the storyboard editor do the rest by choosing Editor ➤ Resolve Auto Layout Issues ➤ Reset to Suggested Constraints in View Controller.

    b. If you tried the preceding step, select Clear Constraints in View Controller again to have a clean start for creating Auto Layout constraints.

Figure 3-13. Two-sided view for compact height (iPhone landscape mode)

7. For the TextField, add the following Auto Layout constraints:

    a. Use Horizontal Center in Container to create an x-alignment constraint with a multiplier of 2.

    b. Use Vertical Center in Container to create a y-alignment constraint with a multiplier of 1.5.

    c. From the top menu bar, select Update Frame at Editor ➤ Resolve Auto Layout Issues.

    d. To update the existing constraints, either select the constraint from the storyboard navigator or select the widget on the scene first to see and click the guided line in the storyboard scene. Use the Attributes Inspector in the Utility area (see Figure 3-14) to update any constraint attribute.

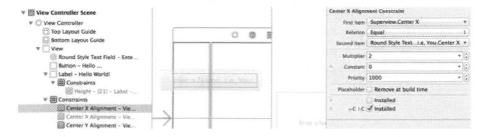

Figure 3-14. Updating the Auto Layout constraint

8. For the Label object, add the following Auto Layout constraints in the same way as in step 7:

   a. Use Horizontal Center in Container to create an x-alignment constraint with a multiplier of 2.

   b. Use Vertical Center in Container to create a y-alignment constraint with a multiplier of 0.75.

   c. From the top menu bar, select Update Frame at Editor ➤ Resolve Auto Layout Issues.

9. For the Button object, add the following Auto Layout constraints in the same way as in step 7:

   a. Use Horizontal Center in Container to create an x-alignment constraint with a multiplier of 0.67.

   b. Use Vertical Center in Container to create a y-alignment constraint with a multiplier of 1.

   c. From the top menu bar, select Update Frame at Editor ➤ Resolve Auto Layout Issues.

All the device classes in previews look good, as expected (Figure 3-15).

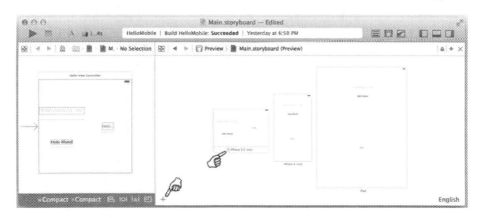

Figure 3-15. Device classes previewed in the storyboard editor

You can run the app in all emulators to see the work in action. Figure 3-16 shows the iPhone 4s emulator. The framework takes care the transition animations for you, too!

Figure 3-16. iPhone 4s portrait and landscape size classes

Content View Controller

WEB ANALOGY

This is the code that is responsible for getting data and injecting it into the template or Document Object Model (DOM) elements.

The Content View Controller participant pairs with a Content View (see Figure 3-1). In the iOS, the Content View normally is created statically in the storyboard. The Content View Controller class manages the Content View to present the dynamic behavior of the user interface by conveying information to and interacting with users. In iOS, you create a custom class by subclassing from UIViewController.

Your primary Content View Controller tasks are as follows:

- Pair with its own Content View
- Keep object references to the UI widgets in the Content View
- Implement methods to respond to widget events

In iOS, you normally use the storyboard editor to connect the UI widgets or events to your code to facilitate these common Content View Controller programming tasks.

Pair with Content View

In iOS, you normally create a storyboard for your apps first (like the iOS HelloMobile project). Generally, for every storyboard scene (Content View), you create a Swift class subclassed from UIViewController to pair with it.

The iOS HelloMobile project is not completed yet; it renders only the initial screen but does not do anything when you click the Hello... button. You need a functional Content View Controller that can fulfill this responsibility. The Single View Application template already pairs a controller class for you: ViewController.swift. To demonstrate the whole subject, don't use this class; instead, do the following to create your own class:

1. Create a new file for a new Swift class.

   a. Right-click the HelloMobile folder in the Navigator area and then select New File ➤ iOS ➤ Source ➤ Swift File (see Figure 2-3).

   b. Save the file as HelloViewController.swift.

   c. Create the HelloViewController class subclassed from UIViewController, as shown in Listing 3-1.

Listing 3-1. HelloViewController Class Skeleton

```
import UIKit
class HelloViewController: UIViewController {
  // TODO
}
```

2. Pair the storyboard scene with the HelloViewController class (see Figure 3-17).

   a. Select Main.storyboard to open the storyboard editor.

   b. Select the view controller in the storyboard scene and open the Identity Inspector in the Utility area.

   c. Enter **HelloViewController** in the Custom Class field to pair the storyboard scene with the HelloViewController class.

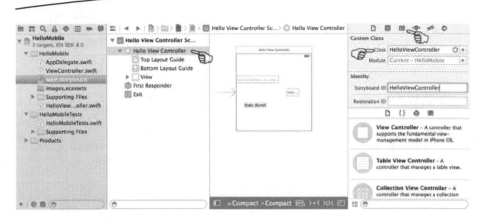

Figure 3-17. Identity Inspector to pair with the view controller

Specifying the custom class in the Identity Inspector is all you need to pair with the Content View Controller.

Interact with Content View

WEB ANALOGY

To interact with an element in a web app, you would attach an event listener, such as onClick(), which would call a function in your controller code.

Generally speaking, you create UI widgets in a Content View, and your Content View Controller code updates the widget's states or interacts with users at runtime. In iOS, you use the Connections Inspector to create IBOutlet and IBAction to facilitate this common programming task by drawing connections to your code in the Swift class.

- ▓ IBOutlet: The view controller property that is connected to the widgets in the storyboard scene

- ▓ IBAction: The view controller method that is called when the widget events occur

The following walks you through the steps to connect the UI widgets and delegates action events to your controller class:

3.   Select Main.storyboard to open the storyboard editor.

    a.   Open the storyboard Assistant Editor. The HelloViewController class should automatically open in the Assistant Editor.

    b.   Sometimes the right file may not be opened automatically in the Assistant Editor, so you may need to select the right file manually (see the pointer in Figure 3-18).

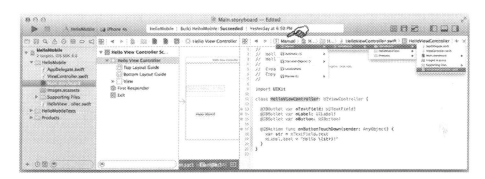

Figure 3-18. Selecting a file manually in the Assistant Editor

4.   Select the TextField in the storyboard scene (the left pointer in Figure 3-19) and open the Connections Inspector (the right pointer in Figure 3-19), as shown in Figure 3-19 (make sure the Utility area is unfolded).

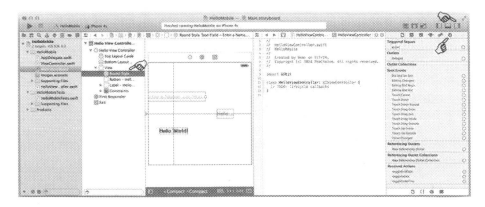

Figure 3-19. Opening the Connections Inspector

5.   Create an IBOutlet for the TextField in the storyboard scene (see Figure 3-20).

   a.   Drag the circle next to New Referencing Outlet with three fingers (or hold the left trackpad button at the same time) and drop it inside the class. You should see the line from the circle, as shown in Figure 3-20.

   b.   Enter the connection name (that is, mTextField). This creates a property in the Swift class.

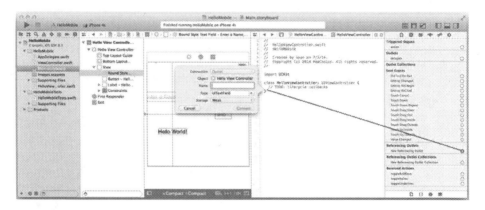

Figure 3-20. IBOutlet in the Connections Inspector

6.   Repeat steps 2 and 3 to create mLabel and mButton IBOutlets.

7.   Create an IBAction for the button touch-down events.

   a.   Drag the circle next to the Touch Down in Sent Events section and drop it inside the Swift class (see Figure 3-21).

   b.   Enter the method name, that is, **onButtonTouchDown**. This creates a method stub in the Swift class.

   c.   Add the Say-Hello code to complete the IBAction method implementation in HelloViewController.swift, as shown in Listing 3-2.

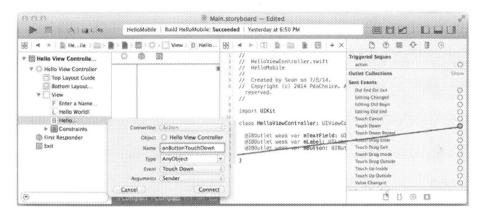

Figure 3-21. *Creating an IBAction in the Connections Inspector*

Listing 3-2. *HelloViewController with IBOutlet and IBAction*

```
import UIKit

class HelloViewController: UIViewController {

  @IBOutlet weak var mTextField: UITextField!
  @IBOutlet weak var mLabel: UILabel!
  @IBOutlet weak var mButton: UIButton!

  @IBAction func onButtonTouchDown(sender: AnyObject) {
    var str = mTextField.text
    mLabel.text = "Hello \(str)!"
  }
}
```

This completes the whole HelloMobile iOS app. You can run the project in all iOS emulators to see the code in action.

You're almost done with the MVC topics. Just one more small lecture before getting into more fun stuff: UIViewController life-cycle events.

UIViewController Life Cycle

┌───┐
│   WEB ANALOGY   │
└───┘

DOM life-cycle events such as DOMContentLoaded, window.onload, or callbacks using jQuery.ready() are typical for web applications that need to manipulate the DOM. To detect when a page is being closed, the window.onbeforeunload event is used.

In iOS apps, life-cycle callbacks are called at various points when a Content View is being rendered. Certain tasks need to be performed in certain states to ensure the Content View is rendered smoothly. This applies to many modem UI platforms including iOS and Android. These events may not be a beginner topic, but the purpose is simple: you want to perform certain computing tasks at the right time to ensure the rendering process is smooth and data is ready at the right time.

Most of these events are optional to implement; you can choose to override these inherited system methods to receive timely callbacks if you want.

viewDidLoad

The iOS system calls the viewDidLoad() method when the view controller loads its Content View. You commonly put the initialization code here.

viewWillAppear

The iOS system calls the viewWillAppear() method when the view is about to appear. Compared to vewDidLoad(), this method gets called every time you revisit the view, while viewDidLoad() gets called only the first time.

viewDidAppear

The iOS system calls the viewDidAppear() method when the view becomes visible. If you want to show rendering effects upon the view being visited, that is, animation effects, you want to put the code in this method. On the other hand, you want to avoid time-consuming code in this method to avoid the UI not being responsive.

viewWillDisappear

The system calls the viewWillDisappear() method when the Content View is about to become invisible—for example, leaving for another storyboard scene. This is usually where you should commit any changes that should be persisted beyond the current user session (because the user might not come back).

viewDidDisappear()

The system calls the viewDidDisappear() method when the Content View is not visible.

When implementing these life-cycle events, you almost always want to call the corresponding super.viewXXX().

Screen Navigation Patterns

You commonly need multiple screens to convey hierarchical information and to interact with users. Considering the relatively small mobile screens, it is more crucial that you use well-known navigation patterns to make mobile apps more predictable. A consistent and predictable navigation pattern guides users to complete a task with multiple screens. Efficient navigation is one of the cornerstones of a well-designed mobile app.

Storyboard Segue

A *segue* (pronounced "seg-way") is a type of a connection in a storyboard that specifies transitions from one scene to another. For instance, you can create an action segue that is performed immediately when the action is triggered. More frequently, you will create a manual segue in storyboard and write logic to perform the segue. Depending on its transition type, the segue may require a Container View Controller. For example, to implement the typical navigation stack transitions, you will need a Navigation Controller in iOS.

The following steps will walk you through creating a storyboard segue:

1. Create a new Xcode project using the Single View Application template with a product name of **Segues**. (See Chapter 2 for step-by-step instructions.)

2. Open `Main.storyboard` in the storyboard editor. It should look like Figure 3-22 when you're done.

    a. Add two Button widgets to the existing scene: one for the action segue and the other for the manual segue.

    b. Drop two View Controller objects onto the storyboard from the Object Library to add two storyboard scenes. Add a UILabel to each scene with the titles **From Action Segue** and **From Manual Segue**.

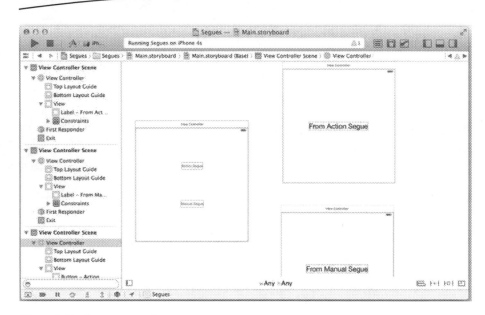

Figure 3-22.   Segue preparation

3. Create an action segue from the Action Segue button to the From Action Segue scene.

    a. Select the Action Segue button and open the Connections Inspector in the Utility area.

    b. Drag the `action` outlet in the Triggered Segue section to the From Action Segue view controller, as shown in Figure 3-23.

    c. Select Show for the transition type.

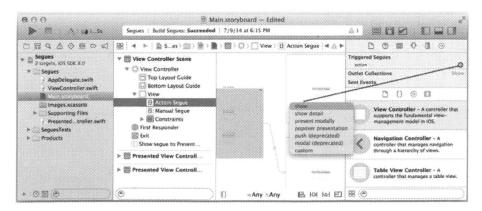

Figure 3-23.   Creating an action segue

4. Select the segue (see the pointer in Figure 3-24) and enter the name of the segue identifier in the segue's Attributes Inspector (that is, type **actionSegue**), as shown in Figure 3-24.

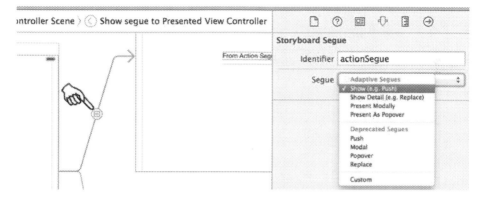

Figure 3-24. Selecting the segue and setting up the attributes

5. Create a Manual Segue from the presenting controller to the From Manual Segue view controller, as shown in Figure 3-25.

   a. Select the presenting view controller and open the Connections Inspector in the Utility area.

   b. Drag the circle (outlet) in the Manual Triggered Segue section to the From Manual Segue view controller.

   c. Select Show for the transition type.

   d. Select the segue and enter the name of the segue identifier in the segue's Attributes Inspector (in other words, type **manualSegue**).

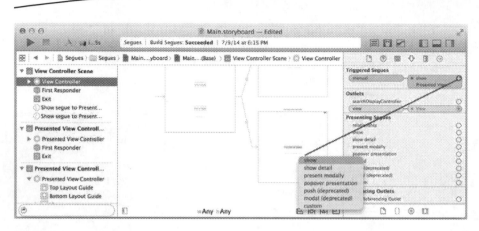

Figure 3-25. Creating a manual segue

6. Set up the manual segue to be performed programmatically when the Manual Segue button is clicked.

a. To connect the button touch down events to your code, create an Touch Down IBAction to the ViewController class with the name onManualSegueTouchDown.

b. In the onManualSegueTouchDown(...) method, use the code in Listing 3-3 to perform the manual segue.

Listing 3-3. Performing the Manual Segue

```
import UIKit
class ViewController: UIViewController {
  @IBAction func onManualSegueTouchDown(sender: AnyObject) {
    self.performSegueWithIdentifier("manualSegue", sender: sender)
  }
}
```

Run the app in different emulators to see these segues work in different size classes. Since iOS 8, the segues are presented in an adaptive manner to the size classes.

Pass Data with a Segue

WEB ANALOGY

Typically, web apps will send requests to the server by passing data through the URL query string, form posting, or cookies. This loads the entire page content for each user action. Single-page front-end apps can utilize animated screen transitions through asynchronous data loading or by front loading more data during their initialization.

The storyboard segues perform screen transitions easily by drawing the segue connections. You don't even need a line of code for an action segue. However, you normally will need to pass data from the presenting view controller to the presented view controller, which cannot be done alone by the storyboard segue itself.

The following steps demonstrate the conventional iOS way to pass data from the presenting view controller to the presented view controller in the Xcode Segues project:

1. Create a PresentedViewController class with a property to receive data. Listing 3-4 simply prints the received data in the viewDidLoad() method.

    a. Specify the PresentedViewController class in the Identity Inspector to pair with the From Action Segue storyboard scene (see the earlier Figure 3-17 for details).

    b. Pair the From Manual Segue storyboard scene with the PresentedViewController class.

    c. Add a property, data, to receive the data from the presenting view controller.

Listing 3-4. Data Property to Receive Data from Presenting View Controller

```
import UIKit
class PresentedViewController: UIViewController {
  var data: String?
  override func viewDidLoad() {
    if let tmp = data {
      println("received data: \(tmp)")
    }
  }
  ...
}
```

2. The system invokes a prepareForSegue(...) method in the source view controller. You need to implement this method to receive the callback. To pass data from the source view controller, ViewController, override the prepareForSegue method, as shown in Listing 3-5.

Listing 3-5. Presenting View Controller Override prepareForSegue

```
override func prepareForSegue(segue: UIStoryboardSegue!, sender: AnyObject!)
{
  var identifier = segue.identifier
  var destVc = (segue.destinationViewController as PresentedViewController)
  destVc.data = "some data from presenting vc \(identifier)"
}
```

Container View Controller

In iOS, screen navigations are primarily implemented by storyboard segues and the Container View Controller classes from the iOS SDK that facilitate the screen navigations. You may create subclasses from these system Container View Controllers, but you normally just use them as is in most of the cases.

> **Note**   Generally speaking, the navigation patterns in this book should appear more familiar to mobile web developers with experience in responsive design or using a mobile framework. For traditional web developers, it is a small investment to get familiar with mobile web development. In addition to HTML5/CSS3, the jQueryMobile and Sencha Touch frameworks are both good choices to leap into this space.

Navigation Stack

The navigation stack is widely used to manage screen transitions, particularly for displaying an information hierarchy, such as a master drill-down list. To show the next screen, push the next view controller into the navigation stack. To go back to the previous screen, pop out the previous view controller from the navigation stack.

You will be guided to create a simple iOS app yourself so you know how to create it and can visualize how it works (see Figure 3-26).

- It has three content views.

- The screen transition is animated that shows the navigation directions.

Figure 3-26. Preview of the iOS NavigationStack app with three screens

In iOS, you draw appropriate storyboard segues with the UINavigationController Container View Controller to accomplish this navigation stack pattern. Let's create a new Xcode project to demonstrate the iOS way.

1. Create a new Xcode project using the iOS Single View Application template (see Chapter 2). Name it **NavigationStack**.

2. Select Main.storyboard to open the storyboard in the Editor area. It has one scene already.

3. Add two more Content View (scenes): drag a View Controller object from the Object Library onto the storyboard twice. Figure 3-27 depicts the storyboard containing three empty scenes.

Figure 3-27.   Three storyboard scenes in the NavigationStack project

4.   Use the preview in Figure 3-26 to guide you as you update the first storyboard scene.

    a.   Add a Label from the Object Library. Change its font size to 30 and text to **Screen One**, and center its alignment with the Attributes Inspector in the Utility area.

    b.   Add Auto Layout constraints to center the label, as shown in Figure 3-28.

    c.   Add the Next button with the right and bottom space constraints to anchor the position, as shown in Figure 3-29.

Figure 3-28.   Screen One label with center constraints

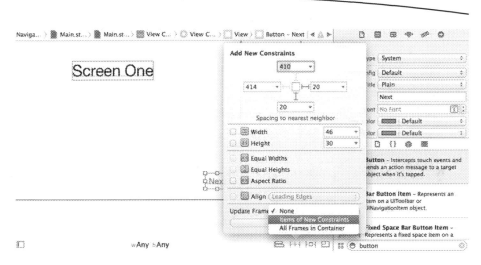

Figure 3-29. Next button with alignment constraints

5. Repeat step 4 to add a Screen Two label and the Next button to the Screen Two scene.

6. Repeat step 4 to add a Screen Three label to the Screen Three scene. Figure 3-30 shows the UI widgets added to storyboard.

Figure 3-30. Three scenes with widgets in NavigationStack project

7. Create an action segue from the Next button in Screen One to the Screen Two scene, and create another action segue from the Next button in Screen Two to the Screen Three scene.

Figure 3-31 shows the results of the storyboard. Run the app to see what is working and what is not working yet. Nothing is new yet; these are the same steps that create storyboard scenes, UI widgets, Auto Layout constraints, and segues that connect them together.

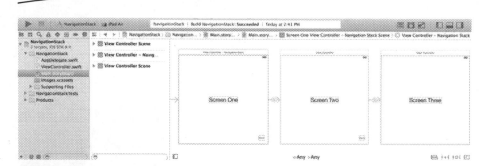

Figure 3-31. NavigationStack storyboard

UINavigationController

The only missing piece in this iOS project is a way to show the appropriate child view controller in the typical push and pop fashions. In iOS, UINavigationController manages the push and pop screen navigation stack behaviors. It also provides a navigation bar that has a default Back button, a title in the center, and an optional right button (see Figure 3-32).

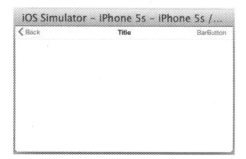

Figure 3-32. The UINavigationController navigation bar

All you need to do is to set up a UINavigationController that associates its root view controller with the first scene.

- Add a Navigation Controller from the Object Library.

- Connect the root view controller segue (in the Connections Inspector) to the first view controller.

You can accomplish both in one simple storyboard operation: embed the Screen One view controller in a Navigation Controller, as shown in the following steps:

1. Select the Screen One view controller from the storyboard.

2. In the Xcode menu bar, select Editor ➤ Embed In ➤ Navigation Controller, as shown in Figure 3-33.

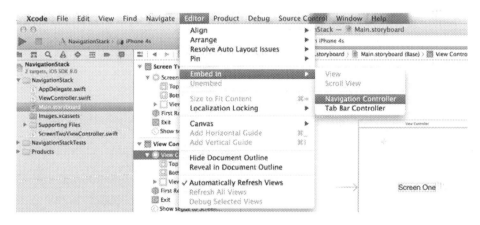

Figure 3-33. Creating a Navigation Controller

3. This creates a Navigation Controller and connects the root view controller segue to the Screen One view controller (see Figure 3-34).

    a. The Navigation Controller has a `NavigationBar`.

    b. The root view controller automatically gets a `NavigationItem` where you can add a center `title` and a `rightBarButtonItem`.

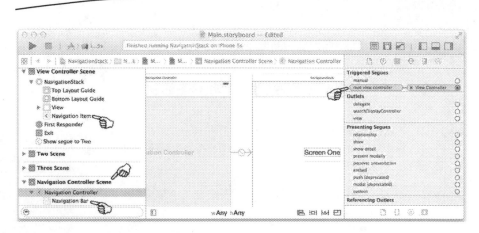

Figure 3-34. Navigation Controller scene and root view controller connection

4. Select the Navigation Item object in Screen One to add title text (that is, type **Navigation Stack**), as shown in Figure 3-35.

   a. The title on the navigation bar also affects the Back button title. iOS automatically updates the button title attribute to reflect where the Back button is going. The button text defaults to Back if the title is not assigned in the view.

Figure 3-35. Title on the Navigation Item

5. Optional: The `title` and the `rightBarButtonItem` need to be installed on Navigation Item, as shown in previous step. If you want to set the `title` attribute or `rightBarButtonItem` to Screen Two or Three, you need to add a Navigation Item to the Screen Two or Three view controller first.

> **Note**   The title can be derived from the view controller title when the Navigation Item is not being configured.

Build and run the app to see the live app in action. You should see that your app looks like Figure 3-26 (shown previously).

Master List with Details Drill-Down

Many apps need to display a list of items that users can select to view more detailed information. They present a master list of items first, and the user selects one item to drill into.

This is probably one of the most common mobile navigation patterns. Most of the popular mobile frameworks including iOS, Android, jQuery mobile, and Sencha Touch mobile JavaScript libraries take care of the memory management for you using recycle views without rendering off-screen list items.

Android and iOS provide guidelines and offer system APIs to promote consistency by making the implementation easy for developers. Both Xcode and the Android IDE supply project templates for creating apps with this UX pattern.

You will create a simple iOS app (see Figure 3-36) to visualize how this works and how to create it.

Figure 3-36. *Preview of the MasterDetail app screens in iOS*

UITableViewController

As you can see in Figure 3-36, this app is purposely simple with two screens only. You need two storyboard scenes: one for the master list and the other for the detailed Content View. To make a fresh start, create a new iOS project.

1.   Launch Xcode, create a new application using the usual Single View Application template, and name it **MasterDetail**.

     a.   You get a `ViewController` class that already pairs with a scene in `Main.storyboard`. Use this pair for the detail view screen.

2. Create the master list storyboard scene and draw a segue to connect the two scenes.

    a. Drag UITableViewController from the Object Library and drop it in the storyboard editor.

    b. Create a Manual Segue from the UITableViewController to the detailed view controller with the Show transition type. Always give the segue an identifier, such as detail (see the earlier Figure 3-25).

3. Select the Table View Cell in the UITableViewController scene and open the Attributes Inspector to configure the Table View Cell (see the pointers in Figure 3-37).

    a. *Style*: Select Basic (or others to see what they are in the editor).

    b. *Identifier*: Enter mycell. Always give the table view cell an identifier. You need it to create reusable cells.

    c. *Accessory*: Select Detail.

    d. Optionally, you can add an image that shows the icon on the left.

Figure 3-37. TableViewCell attributes

4. Embed the UITableViewController in a Navigation Controller (see the earlier Figure 3-33). You normally use a navigation stack pattern for the screen transitions.

5. Check the Is the Initial View Controller in the Navigation Controller Attributes Inspector (see Figure 3-38) to make the Navigation Controller the starting view controller of this app.

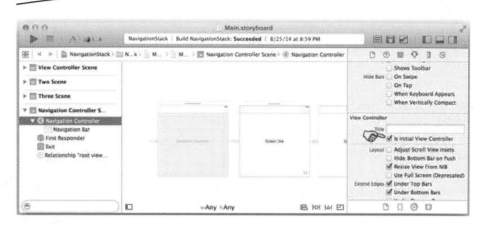

Figure 3-38. MasterDetail storyboard

6.   Create a MasterTableViewController Swift class in the
     ViewController.swift file, as shown in Listing 3-6.

     a.   Subclass MasterTableViewController from
          UITableViewController.

     b.   Pair this MasterTableViewController class with the
          Table View Controller scene in the Identity Inspector
          (see the earlier Figure 3-17).

Listing 3-6. MasterListTableViewController Class

```
class MasterTableViewController : UITableViewController {
  // TODO
}
```

Note   In Swift, the class doesn't need to be in its own file. I chose to put
it in the existing ViewController.swift file for no particular reason.

UITableViewDataSource

To populate the items in the Table View, UITableView, you implement a data source. Specifically, you provide the TableViewCell with data by overriding the methods defined in the UITableViewDataSource protocol (see Listing 3-7). Do the following in the MasterDetail project:

1. Implement tableView(tableView, numberOfRowsInSec tion) to return the number of items in the tableView.

2. Implement tableView(tableView, cellForRowAtIndexPath) to return the tableViewCell instance.

Listing 3-7. Implement UITableViewDataSource Protocol

```
class MasterTableViewController : UITableViewController {
  var items = ["item 1", "item 2", "item 3"]

  override func tableView(tableView: UITableView, numberOfRowsInSection
section: Int) -> Int {
    return self.items.count
  }

  override func tableView(tableView: UITableView, cellForRowAtIndexPath
indexPath: NSIndexPath) -> UITableViewCell {
    var cell = tableView.dequeueReusableCellWithIdentifier("mycell") as
UITableViewCell
    cell.textLabel!.text = self.items[indexPath.row]
    return cell
  }
}
```

> **Note**   Use dequeueReusableCellWithIdentifier(...) to implement recycled views. This is a common pattern for saving memory with a large number of items, and iOS makes it easy by offering this method. Make sure you assign a cell identifier to the table view cell in the storyboard.

UITableViewDelegate

To handle table view item selected events, override the UITableViewDelegate.tableView(tableView, didSelectRowAtIndexPath) method (see Listing 3-8).

1. Implement `UITableViewDelegate`.
    `didSelectRowAtIndexPath(...)` to perform segues.

2. Implement a `prepareForSegue(...)` callback to pass
    data to the detail view controller (see Listing 3-5 for
    details).

Listing 3-8. Implementing UITableViewDelegate

```
class MasterTableViewController : UITableViewController {
  ...
  override func tableView(tableView: UITableView, didSelectRowAtIndexPath
indexPath: NSIndexPath) {
    self.performSegueWithIdentifier("detail", sender:
    indexPath.row)
  }

  override func prepareForSegue(segue: UIStoryboardSegue,
  sender: AnyObject) {
    var destVc = segue.destinationViewController as
    UIViewController
    destVc.navigationItem.title = self.items[sender as Int]
  }
```

3. After adding or deleting items, you need to explicitly
    refresh the table view.

    a. Drag a Bar Button Item object to the navigation bar and
        draw an `IBAction` to create the `doAdd()` method
        (Figure 3-39).

    b. To add an item when the Add button is selected,
        implement the `doAdd()` method, as shown in Listing 3-9. Make
        sure you call `TableView.reloadData()` in the main thread to
        refresh the table.

Listing 3-9. Refresh Table View

```
class MasterTableViewController : UITableViewController {
  var items = ["item 1", "item 2", "item 3"]

  @IBAction func doAdd(sender: AnyObject) {
    self.items.append("item \(self.items.count + 1)")
    self.tableView.reloadData()
  }
  ...
```

Figure 3-39. Navigation bar right button

Build and run (⌘+R) the app to see the MasterDetail iOS app in action.
You should see that your app looks like the preview shown previously in
Figure 3-36.

UITableView

Previously, you used `UITableViewController`, which is a regular
`UIViewController` with a prewired `tableView` object in it. The prewired
`tableView` also prewires the `dataSource` and `delegate` to the host
`UITableViewController`, which simplifies some coding for you (actually
not that much, in my opinion). The prewired `tableView` takes up the whole
screen, which may not be what you want. More often, I choose to do the
following instead of using `UITableViewController`.

1. In the storyboard, create a regular `ViewController`
   with `TableView`.

   a. Add a regular `View Controller` scene.

   b. Add a table view to the scene. This gives you more
      flexibility (that is, to draw the table view at any
      location and size).

   c. Connect the table view to an `IBOutlet` (see the earlier
      Figure 3-20 for details).

   d. Select the `table view` and connect `delegate` and
      `dataSource` outlets to the `ViewController` in the
      Connection Inspector.

2. Create a Swift class to pair with the Content View.

   a. Subclass from the regular `UIViewController` class.

   b. Implement the `UITableViewDataSource` and
      `UITableViewDelegate` protocols.

The previous `MasterTableViewController` is essentially equivalent to the
code in Listing 3-10, and you still implement the same methods declared in
`UITableViewDataSource` and `UITableViewDelegate`.

Listing 3-10. Explicitly Implement Table View Protocols

```
class MasterTableViewController2 : UIViewController, UITableViewDataSource,
UITableViewDelegate {
  @IBOutlet weak var tableView: UITableView!
  ...
```

UITableViewCell

In iOS, the line items in the UITableView are called *cells*. You get some
free types of UITableViewCell that you can select from the iOS SDK.
Previously in the MasterDetail project, you selected the Basic style,
which gives you one textLabel in the Table View cell (see Figure 3-37).
Right Details, Left Details, or Subtitle styles all give you a second label
called detailedTextLabel. You can also set a left image icon and other
TableViewCell attributes, as shown in Figure 3-37.

Still, it is the data source's responsibility to render the cell with data: You
programmatically bind each UITableViewCell with data by implementing
the tableView(cellForRowAtIndexPath) method. Listing 3-11 shows a
typical example.

Listing 3-11. TableViewCell Properties

```
override func tableView(tableView: UITableView, cellForRowAtIndexPath
indexPath: NSIndexPath) -> UITableViewCell {
  var cell = ...
  cell.textLabel!.text = self.items[indexPath.row]
  cell.detailTextLabel!.text = "some detail label"
  cell.imageView!.image = UIImage(named: "pointer.png")
  cell.accessoryType = UITableViewCellAccessoryType.DetailButton
  return cell
}
```

You can also choose the Custom style and draw the cell freely using the
storyboard; you will do so in the next section.

UICollectionView

The MasterDetail project you created fits comfortably on an iPhone, but
when it is running on the iPad, it feels like the space is not being utilized
efficiently. On iOS platforms, UICollectionView comes to the rescue: it
allows multiple columns to organize the master list items, rather than a
simple one-dimensional list.

It would be a shame if you didn't try this variant right now because it
is a really useful widget that takes very little extra effort. The key is the
UICollectionView class.

> **Note** You can also use `UICollectionViewController`, which contains a `UICollectionView` that occupies the whole scene by default. Same choice: `UITableViewController` versus `UITableView`, which was discussed earlier (see the "UITableView" section).

Create a new Xcode project using `UICollectionView` to demonstrate the usage.

1. Launch Xcode and create a new application using the usual Single View Application template. Name it **MasterGridDetail**.

    a. You get a scene in the `Main.storyboard` file and a `ViewController` class pair.

    b. Rename the class to `MasterViewController` in the `ViewController.swift` file and as the custom class name of the view controller scene (see Figure 3-17).

    c. Drag a Collection View from the Object Library and drop it onto the `MasterViewController` scene. Let it take up the whole space and pin zero spacing to the Superview in all four directions from the Xcode menu bar by selecting Editor ➤ Pin.

    d. Embed the `MasterViewController` controller in the Navigation Controller (see Figure 3-33).

2. Select the Collection View in the storyboard to create connections in the Connections Inspector, as shown in Figure 3-40.

    a. Connect the `dataSource` and `delegate` outlets to the `MasterViewController`.

    b. Open the Assistant Editor and connect the New Referencing Outlet to the `MasterViewController` property. Enter **mCollectionView** for its name.

Figure 3-40. Collection View dataSource, delegate, and IBOutlet connections

3. Draw your own custom collection view cell in the storyboard.

    a. In the Attributes Inspector, assign the Collection Reusable View Cell Identifier a value (mycell). There are some attributes you can change safely in the Attributes Inspector, such as the white background color.

    b. To change the size of the cell, select the parent collection view and change the cell size to 150 × 150 in the Size Inspector. Figure 3-41 shows other measurements that you can set.

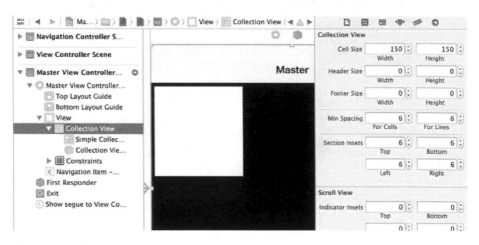

Figure 3-41. Size Inspector

    c. Add a label to the cell, make the font size bigger (that is, 30), use center alignment, and add Auto Layout constraints, as shown in Figure 3-42.

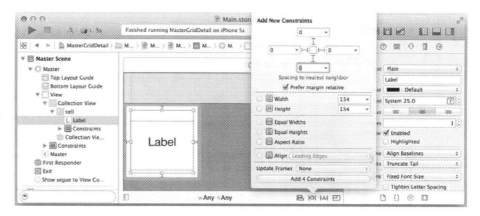

Figure 3-42. Drawing the collection view cell

4. Create a custom Swift class for the collection view cell. Listing 3-12 shows the `SimpleCollectionViewCell` class.

   a. Create a Swift class, `SimpleCollectionViewCell`, subclassed from `UICollectionViewCell`.

   b. Select the collection view cell in the storyboard and assign the `SimpleCollectionViewCell` class in the Identity Inspector.

   c. Open the Assistant Editor with the `SimpleCollectionViewCell` class. In the Connections Inspector, connect the referencing outlet to create an `IBOutlet`, and name it **textLabel**.

Listing 3-12. SimpleCollectionViewCell Class

```
class SimpleCollectionViewCell : UICollectionViewCell {
  @IBOutlet weak var textLabel: UILabel!
}
```

5. Create the detail view controller scene in the storyboard, as shown Figure 3-43.

   a. Add a regular view controller from the Object Library.

   b. Create a manual segue from the Master View Controller scene to the detailed view controller with a Show transition type (see Figure 3-25). Always enter a storyboard segue Identifier (detail).

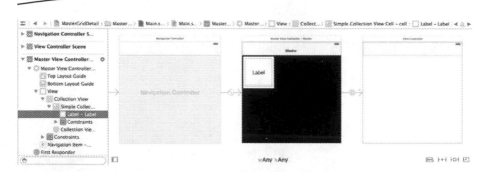

Figure 3-43. Creating the detail view controller in MasterDetail storyboard

6. MasterViewController must implement
    the UICollectionViewDataSource and
    UICollectionViewDelegate protocols (see Listing 3-13).

    a. Implement numberOfSectionsInCollectionView
        (collectionView) to return the section number;
        it defaults to 1 if not implemented.

    b. Implement collectionView(collectionView,
        numberOfItemsInSection) to return the number of items
        in each section.

    c. Implement collectionView(collectionView,
        cellForItemAtIndexPath) to return the collection
        view cell instance.

    d. Implement collectionView(collectionView,
        didSelectItemAtIndexPath) to respond to the cell selection.

Listing 3-13. UICollectionViewDataSource and UICollectionViewDelegate Protocols

```
class MasterViewController : UIViewController, UICollectionViewDataSource,
UICollectionViewDelegate {
  ...
  // implement UICollectionViewDataSource
  var items = ["item 1", "item 2", "item 3", "item 4", "item 5", "item 6",
"item 7"]
  func collectionView(collectionView: UICollectionView,
numberOfItemsInSection section: Int) -> Int {
    return self.items.count
  }

  // The cell that is returned must be retrieved from a call to -dequeueReus
ableCellWithReuseIdentifier:forIndexPath:
  func collectionView(collectionView: UICollectionView,
cellForItemAtIndexPath indexPath: NSIndexPath) -> UICollectionViewCell {
```

```
    var cell = collectionView.dequeueReusableCellWithReuseIdentifier("cell",
forIndexPath: indexPath) as SimpleCollectionViewCell
    cell.textLabel.text = self.items[indexPath.row]
    cell.backgroundColor = (indexPath.row % 2 == 0) ? UIColor.whiteColor() :
UIColor.lightGrayColor()
    return cell
  }

  func numberOfSectionsInCollectionView(collectionView: UICollectionView) ->
Int {
    return 1
  }

  // implement UICollectionViewDelegate
  func collectionView(collectionView: UICollectionView,
didSelectItemAtIndexPath indexPath: NSIndexPath) {
    self.performSegueWithIdentifier("detail", sender: self)
  }
}
```

Both TableView and CollectionView are versatile. You should look into the data source and delegate protocols to see the rich options offered to developers. Build and run the MasterGridDetail iOS app to see your code live in action, as shown in Figure 3-44.

Figure 3-44. Collection view

Navigation Tabs

Navigation tabs are another popular UX design pattern. Apple's iOS Human Interface Guidelines suggest using a tab bar to give users access to different perspectives on the same set of data or on different subtasks related to the overall function of your app. Each navigation tab is associated with a view controller. When the user selects a specific tab, the associated view controller presents its own Content View.

Not only does this pattern exist in iOS, but it also widely used in many mobile platforms. You may simply call it *tabs* in desktop or web apps.

You will create a simple tabbed iOS app (see Figure 3-45) to visualize how this works and how to create it.

Figure 3-45. Preview of the iOS TabbedApp

The key in iOS is the Container View Controller, which is the UITabBarController class. You can use it as is most of the time. If you want to keep some application states in the Container View Controller, simply subclass from it.

Implementing Navigation Tabs

The following instructions walk you through the steps you normally take to implement navigation tabs:

1. Launch Xcode to create a new app using the Single View Application template and name it **TabbedApp**.

    a. You get an empty scene in the Main.storyboard and a ViewController class.

    b. Rename the class to FirstViewController in both the ViewController.swift file and the class name in the Identity Inspector for the storyboard scene.

    c. Draw the Content View in the storyboard scene using the Android app as your wireframe.

2. You need the second Content View and view controller pair.

    a. You can copy, paste, and modify from the FirstViewController class. Listing 3-14 shows the SecondViewController class.

Listing 3-14. SecondViewController Class

```
class SecondViewController: UIViewController {
    ...
}
```

    b. You can copy, paste, and modify the storyboard scene in the storyboard editor, too. Don't forget to update the class name in the Identify Inspector. Figure 3-46 shows that the storyboard has the Screen One and Screen Two scenes.

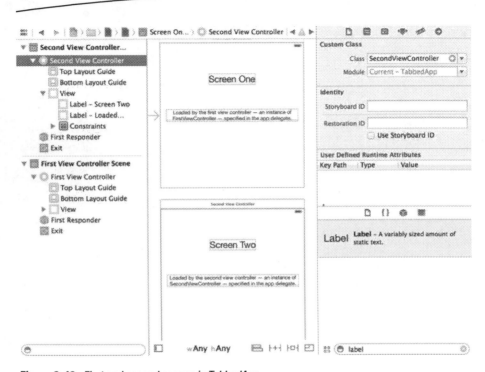

Figure 3-46. First and second scenes in TabbedApp

3. Add a Container View Controller, UITabBarController, which will be responsible for managing the two Content View Controllers.

    c. Embed both storyboard scenes in a TabBarController: multiselect both storyboard scenes (press and hold the ⌘ key for multiselect) and select the command from Editor ➤ Embed In ➤ Tab Bar Controller in the Xcode menu bar (see Figure 3-47).

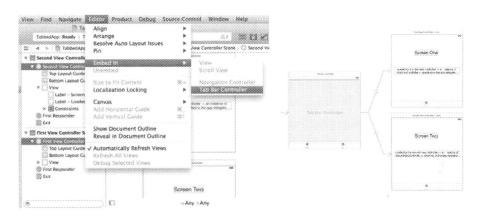

Figure 3-47. Embed Content Views in Tab Bar Controller (the result on the right)

The app is not complete yet, but you actually can run it now to see the app live. It should look like the preview shown in Figure 3-45.

UITabBarController

As you can see from the previous work (see Figure 3-45), a bottom tab bar comes with UITabBarController. Each tab bar item is associated with a Content View Controller. By selecting a tab bar item, the UITabBarController automatically presents the selected Content View Controller.

Add/Remove a Tab Bar Item

UITabBarController maintains an array of references to its child view controllers. In its Connections Inspector, you can draw a view controller's outlet in the Triggered Segues section to add the child view controllers to the UITabBarController.viewControllers array property. You can write code to add or remove the child view controller in the runtime, but doing so in a storyboard is easier and more robust for creating static tabs.

Update the Look and Feel of the Tab Bar Items

You should assign a title and an image to the tab bar items. When a UIViewController is added to a tab bar controller, the UIViewController. tabBarItem property represents the tab bar item in the tab bar. You assign appropriate values in the tab bar item's Attributes Inspector. In the runtime, you use code to update the text and image by setting appropriate tabBarItem properties. Figure 3-48 shows two tab bar items with the same label and without an icon image. Do the following to give your TabbedApp a better look:

1. System provides a set of common tab bar items (System Item in the Attributes Inspector). Use them when possible for consistent platform convention. Select the Featured system item for Screen One (see Figure 3-48).

Figure 3-48. Adding the Featured system item to Screen One

2. For Screen Two, select Custom to supply your own tab bar item title and image icon (see Figure 3-49).

    a. Enter **Two** for the title.

    b. Create an image icon in images.xcassets (in other words, tab1) and drop a transparent PNG with size about 25 × 25 (maximum 48 × 32). The icon color is not required because only the alpha channel is to be rendered.

Note   iOS is picky about the right image specs. See the online reference for image specs: https://developer.apple.com/library/ios/ documentation/UserExperience/Conceptual/MobileHIG/ IconMatrix.html.

---

    c. Enter the image name (for example, tab1).

    d. You may enter a badge (for example, New), which will appear in the upper-right corner of the icon. Frequently, it is set programmatically in the runtime using the UITabbatItem.badgeValue property.

Figure 3-49. Custom tab item with badgeValue

Handle Runtime Behavior

To respond to the runtime behavior programatically, just like most of the UIKit widgets, you implement a delegate protocol: UITabBarDelegate. Continue with the TabbedApp to learn the common tasks for handling UITabBarDelegate runtime events.

1. Create a custom tab bar controller to handle runtime behaviors, as shown in Listing 3-15.

    a. Create a SimpleTabBarController class subclassing from UITabBarController.

    b. Declare SimpleTabBarController to implement the UITabBarControllerDelegate protocol.

    c. In the storyboard, select the tab bar controller and assign the SimpleTabBarController class in the Identity Inspector.

Listing 3-15. SimpleTabBarController Class

```
class SimpleTabBarController : UITabBarController,
UITabBarControllerDelegate {
  override func viewDidLoad() {
    super.viewDidLoad()
    // Do any additional setup after loading the view ...
    self.delegate = self
  }

  func tabBarController(tabBarController: UITabBarController!,
shouldSelectViewController viewController: UIViewController!) -> Bool {
    // you may do something and return true
    // Or, return false to not to select viewController
    return false;
  }
```

```
  func tabBarController(tabBarController: UITabBarController!,
didSelectViewController viewController: UIViewController!) {
    // you may do something
  }
}
```

2. Each child Content View Controller can access
   the UIViewController.tabBarController and
   UIViewController.tabBarItem properties.
   Listing 3-16 shows how to change the second tab's
   badgeValue from the FirstViewController.

Listing 3-16. Change badgeValue of Other tabBarItem

```
(self.tabBarController!.viewControllers![1] as UIViewController).tabBarItem.
badgeValue = "Zzz"
```

By the way, the tab bar is located on the bottom screen in iOS instead of
at the top in Android or many web sites. In general, platform-specific UX
guidelines should never be overlooked. Keep the navigation bar on the
bottom in iOS, which is where most iOS users expect it.

Swipe Views

The carousel is a popular UX pattern commonly used in many platforms,
including desktop and web apps. On mobile platforms, you use this pattern
with swipe gestures to display content page by page. It allows the user
to move from item to item efficiently. With animated transitions, it offers a
more enjoyable viewing experience. Both iOS and many JavaScript libraries
provide framework classes or APIs, as well as a project creation template to
promote this navigation UX pattern.

You will be guided to create a simple SwipeViews iOS app (see Figure 3-50)
to visualize how this works and how to create it.

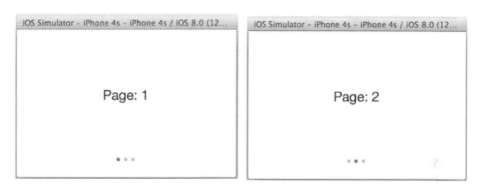

Figure 3-50. Preview of the iOS SwipeViews app

As usual for a top-down approach, you want to construct the storyboard scenes to start.

1.   Launch Xcode to create a new project using the usual Single View Application template and name it **SwipeViews**.

2.   Rename the existing class ViewController to ParentViewController in both the ViewController. swift file and the custom class name in the Identity Inspector of the view controller's storyboard scene.

3.   Drag and drop a UIView onto the storyboard scene from the Object Library.

   a.   Open the storyboard Assistant Editor, create an IBOutlet in the Connections Inspector by connecting the referencing outlet to the paired view controller, and name it **mPageView**.

   b.   Add Auto Layout constraints to pin the edges to the nearest neighbors and set the background to be light gray.

4.   You need another Content View–view controller pair for the page content.

   a.   Create a new PageContentViewController class (see Listing 3-17).

Listing 3-17. Two Classes in ViewController.swift File

```
import UIKit
class ParentViewController : UIViewController {
  @IBOutlet weak var mPageView: UIView!

  override func viewDidLoad() {
```

```
   super.viewDidLoad()
 }

 override func didReceiveMemoryWarning() {
   super.didReceiveMemoryWarning()
   // Dispose of any resources that can be recreated.
 }
}

class PageContentViewController: UIViewController {
 @IBOutlet weak var textLabel : UILabel!
}
```

    b.   Draw the second storyboard scene (see the screen on the right in Figure 3-51). Make sure you give the Page Content View Controller a storyboard ID (such as `PageContentViewController`). You need the ID to programmatically load a view controller from the storyboard.

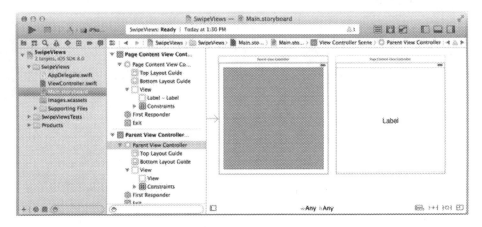

Figure 3-51. Main.storyboard in SwipeViews project

Nothing is new yet; you just drew two storyboard scenes with the view controllers to start with. You may build and run the app to make sure it contains no errors. Unlike previous navigation stack or tab patterns to which you can draw segues for view controller transitions, you need to write code to complete the app, which you will do next.

UIPageViewController

The key to implementing the swipe view UX pattern in iOS is the UIPageViewController class, which uses the same data source pattern: you implement a data source that is responsible for providing Content Views populated with data. Continue with the following steps in the SwipeViews Xcode project:

1. Modify the PageContentViewController class so it can receive data and present the three simple screens (see Listing 3-18).

Listing 3-18. Add the data and pageNo Properties

```
class PageContentViewController: UIViewController {

  @IBOutlet weak var textLabel : UILabel!

  var data = ""
  var pageNo = 0

  override func viewDidLoad() {
    self.textLabel.text = data
  }
}
```

2. UIPageViewController works with the dataSource and delegate protocols. The parent view controller, ParentViewController, is a legitimate candidate for implementing them (see Listing 3-19).

    a. UIPageViewControllerDataSource is responsible for supplying the Content View Controller before and after the current content one.

    b. UIPageViewControllerDataSource also defines the optional page count and page selection indicator.

    c. UIPageViewControllerDelegate protocol defines the optional page view controller callback methods.

Listing 3-19. ParentViewController Implements dataSource and delegate Protocol

```
class ParentViewController : UIViewController,
UIPageViewControllerDataSource, UIPageViewControllerDelegate {

  ...
  // implement data source
  let items = ["Page: 1", "Page: 2", "Page: 3"]
```

```
    func pageViewController(pageViewController: UIPageViewController,
viewControllerBeforeViewController viewController: UIViewController) ->
UIViewController? {

        var pageNo = (viewController as PageContentViewController).pageNo
        if pageNo > 0 {
          var vc = self.storyboard!.
instantiateViewControllerWithIdentifier("PageContentViewController") as
PageContentViewController
            vc.data = self.items[pageNo-1]
            vc.pageNo = pageNo - 1
            return vc
        }

        return nil
    }

    func pageViewController(pageViewController: UIPageViewController,
viewControllerAfterViewController viewController: UIViewController) ->
UIViewController? {

        var pageNo = (viewController as PageContentViewController).pageNo
        if pageNo < self.items.count - 1 {
          var vc = self.storyboard!.
instantiateViewControllerWithIdentifier("PageContentViewController") as
PageContentViewController
            vc.data = self.items[pageNo+1]
            vc.pageNo = pageNo + 1
            return vc
        }

        return nil
    }

    func presentationCountForPageViewController(pageViewController:
UIPageViewController) -> Int {
        return self.items.count
    }

    func presentationIndexForPageViewController(pageViewController:
UIPageViewController) -> Int {
        return (pageViewController.viewControllers[0] as
PageContentViewController).pageNo
    }
    ...
```

3. In the `ParentViewController` `viewDidLoad()` method,
   the following conventional code (see Listing 3-20)
   sets up the `UIPageViewController`:

   a. Initialize the page view controller.

   b. Set up the `dataSource` and delegate.

   c. Set up the first page view controller.

   d. Establish the parent-child view controller hierarchy.

Listing 3-20. Setting Up UIPageViewController in viewDidLoad

```
class ParentViewController : UIViewController,
UIPageViewControllerDataSource, UIPageViewControllerDelegate {

  @IBOutlet weak var mPageView: UIView!
  var mPageViewController: UIPageViewController!

  override func viewDidLoad() {
    super.viewDidLoad()
    // Do any additional setup after loading the view, typically from a nib.

    // a. initialize page view controller, view and gestures
    self.mPageViewController = UIPageViewController(transitionStyl
e: UIPageViewControllerTransitionStyle.Scroll, navigationOrientation:
UIPageViewControllerNavigationOrientation.Horizontal, options: nil)
    self.mPageViewController.view.frame = self.mPageView.bounds
    self.mPageView.gestureRecognizers = self.mPageViewController.
gestureRecognizers

    // b. set data source and delegate
    self.mPageViewController!.delegate = self
    self.mPageViewController!.dataSource = self

    // c. set the first page
    var vc = self.storyboard!.
instantiateViewControllerWithIdentifier("PageContentViewController") as
PageContentViewController
    vc.data = self.items[0]
    vc.pageNo = 0
    self.mPageViewController.setViewControllers([vc], direction: .Forward,
animated: false, completion: nil)

    // d. establish parent-child view and view controller hierachy
    self.mPageView.addSubview(self.mPageViewController.view)
    self.addChildViewController(self.mPageViewController)
    self.mPageViewController.didMoveToParentViewController(self)
  }
  ...
```

This is all about the `UIPageViewController` class and the swipe view navigation pattern in iOS. Build and run the iOS SwipeViews app to see your code in action. It should look like the preview shown in Figure 3-50.

Dialogs

Generally, you use the dialogs UX pattern to give users quick feedback or to request a simple confirmation of choices. Dialogs normally sit on top of the current screen while that screen remains partially visible or dimmed. This creates a visual effect that is meant to get more user attention without losing the current context.

Create an Xcode project to demonstrate the uses of dialogs and common programming tasks.

1. Launch Xcode to create a new project using the Single View Application template and name it **Dialogs**.

2. Draw two Button widgets with titles set to `Alert` and `Popup` in the storyboard scene, as shown in Figure 3-52.

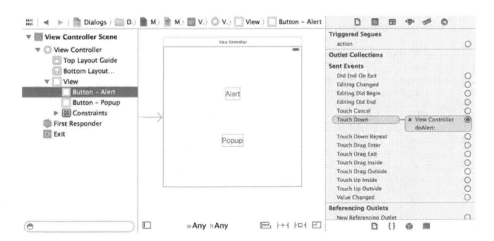

Figure 3-52. Dialogs storyboard

3. Open the storyboard Assistant Editor and connect the Send Event ➤ Touch Down outlet in the Connections Inspector to create IBAction methods in the paired ViewController class for both buttons (see doAlert(...) and doPopup(...) in Listing 3-21).

Listing 3-21. Create IBAction Methods for the Alert and Pop-up Buttons

```
import UIKit
class ViewController: UIViewController, UIAlertViewDelegate {
  ...
  @IBAction func doAlert(sender: AnyObject) {
    // TODO
  }
  @IBAction func doPopup(sender: AnyObject) {
    // TODO
  }
}
```

Nothing should be new to you here, but this Dialogs Xcode project should give you a refresher on dialog topics.

UIAlertController

WEB ANALOGY

The window.alert() method halts code execution and offers only one action for the user: to close the alert dialog and continue.

Figure 3-53 shows the standard Android and iOS alert dialogs side by side. On iOS, you use UIAlertController that replaces UIAlertView since iOS 8.

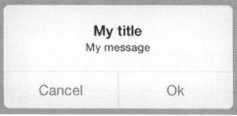

Figure 3-53. Android (left) and iOS (right) alert dialogs

Contiune with the Xcode Dialogs project and add the following code to learn the UIAlertController code:

1. To show the iOS dialog as depicted in Figure 3-53, add the following code in the ViewController.doAlert(...) method (see Listing 3-22):

    a. Create a UIAlertController instance.

    b. Add UIAlertAction for dialog buttons.

    c. To prompt user input, add TextField to UIAlertController.

    d. Use the regular UIViewController API to present it as a view controller.

Listing 3-22. Present UIAlertController

```
@IBAction func doAlert(sender: AnyObject) {

  var alert = UIAlertController(title: "My title", message: "My message",
preferredStyle: UIAlertControllerStyle.Alert)

  // add action buttons
  var actionCancel = UIAlertAction(title: "Cancel", style:
UIAlertActionStyle.Cancel,
      handler: {action in
        // do nothing
      })

    var actionOk = UIAlertAction(title: "Ok", style: UIAlertActionStyle.
Default,
      handler: {action in
        println((alert.textFields![0] as UITextField).text)
      })

  alert.addAction(actionCancel)
  alert.addAction(actionOk)

  // add text fields
  alert.addTextFieldWithConfigurationHandler({textField in
    // config the UITextField
    textField.backgroundColor = UIColor.yellowColor()
    textField.placeholder = "enter text, i.e., Do Ra Me"
    })

  // UIViewController API to presend viewController
  self.presentViewController(alert, animated: true, completion: nil)
}
```

Everything inside UIAlertController is created programatically. Figure 3-54 shows the UIAlertController code in action.

Figure 3-54. Android iOS UIAlertController

UIPopoverController

On iOS devices with large screens such as the iPad, you can use PopoverController to present a regular viewController as a pop-over. The pop-over can be anchored at a given position to associate the presented dialog with the presenting context. On devices with compact size classes such as the iPhone, the pop-over controller automatically falls back to the regular full-screen view controller. You can also take advantage of the storyboard editor to draw the Content Views and segue instead of writing code.

The following steps demonstrate how to use PopoverController in the Dialogs project:

1.   Add a new storyboard scene for the pop-over Content View (see Figure 3-55).

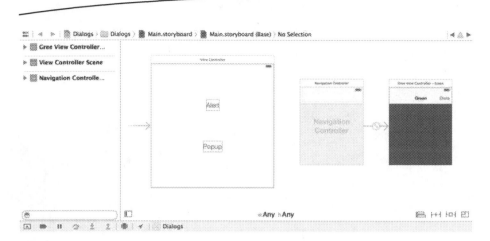

Figure 3-55. Dialogs storyboard completion

    a.   Create a `GreenViewController` class, as shown in Listing 3-23, and draw a view controller scene in the storyboard to pair with it by specifying the class name in the Identity Inspector.

Listing 3-23. GreenViewController Class

```
class GreenViewController : UIViewController {
  @IBAction func doDone(sender: AnyObject) {
    // do something and dismiss
    self.dismissViewControllerAnimated(true, completion:nil)
  }
}
```

    b.   Embed the view controller in a Navigation Controller (Editor ➤ Embed in from the Xcode menu bar) to take advantage of the navigation bar title or any Navigation Controller features.

    c.   In the Navigation Controller Attributes Inspector, change the Simulated Metrics Size value to Freeform; then change the Simulated Size value to 250 × 300 in the Size Inspector.

    d.   In the Navigation Controller Identity Inspector, specify the storyboard ID as **nav**. You always need the ID if you want to instantiate a view controller instance directly from a storyboard (see Listing 3-24).

e. You normally draw meaningful contents in a Content View. For simplicity, use the Attributes Inspector to change the `GreenViewController` view's Background attribute to Green.

f. Draw a `BarButtonItem` on the right side of navigation bar in the `GreenViewController` and connect the Send Actions outlet to the `IBAction` method in `GreenViewController`, as shown in Listing 3-23. Figure 3-55 depicts the completed storyboard.

2. To present the `GreenViewController`, draw a manual segue from the presenting `ViewController` to the parent Navigation Controller of `GreenViewController`. Specify the segue attribute values as shown in the Attributes Inspector in Figure 3-56.

a. *Identifier*: Set this to **mypopover**.

b. *Segue type*: Set this to **Present As Popover**.

c. *Direction*: Set this to Up (you may play with other values).

d. *Anchor outlet*: Drag the outlet to the Popup button in the presenting view controller.

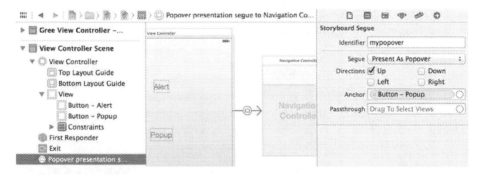

Figure 3-56. Storyboard segue attributes in the Attributes Inspector

3. To perform the `mypopover` manual segue, update the `ViewController.doPopup(...)` `IBAction` method as shown in Listing 3-24. Note that the commented code programmatically presents a `UIPopoverController` without using the storyboard segue.

Listing 3-24. Perform the mypopover Manual Segue

```
// In ViewController class
@IBAction func doPopup(sender: AnyObject) {
  self.performSegueWithIdentifier("mypopover", sender: nil)

// var nav = self.storyboard!.instantiateViewControllerWithIdentifier("nav")
as UIViewController
// var popover = UIPopoverController(contentViewController: nav)
// popover.delegate = self;
// popover.popoverContentSize = nav.view.bounds.size
// popover.presentPopoverFromRect(self.mPopupButton.frame, inView: self.
view, permittedArrowDirections: UIPopoverArrowDirection.Up, animated: true)
}
```

4.   You can dismiss the pop-over by tapping anywhere inside the presenting view controller but outside the GreenViewController Content View. To dismiss the pop-over programmatically, implement GreenViewController.doDone(...) to call the dismissViewControllerAnimated(...), as shown in Listing 3-23.

You can build and run the Xcode Dialogs project to see the UIPopoverController code in action. UIPopoverController is rendered as a pop-up dialog on an iPad, while the same code renders a full-screen modal screen in compact-sized classes such as the iPhone, as shown in Figure 3-57.

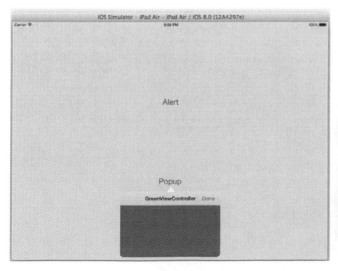

Figure 3-57. The results of the UIPopoverController code on the iPad vs. the iPhone

Summary

To start developing an iOS app, first create storyboard scenes using the wireframe or mock-up to break your app naturally into a structured MVC project in a top-down fashion. The result is a set of Content View–View Controller pairs.

Next, to implement the screen navigation patterns, you draw storyboard segues to connect storyboard scenes. You also choose the appropriate Container View Controller (such as `UINavigationController`) from the SDK to facilitate the screen transitions. You will dive into the details of each screen in Chapter 4.

Implement Piece by Piece

In the previous chapter, you used an iOS storyboard to lay the groundwork for using navigation patterns. It resulted in a set of connected `UIViewController` classes in a model-view-controller (MVC) framework that mapped to Android counterpart fragments.

In this chapter, you will implement each view-controller pair one piece at a time. You will also focus on the following common programming-task mappings from iOS to Android:

- User interface and common UI widgets

- Persistent storage options

- Network and remote services with JavaScript Object Notation (JSON)

User Interface

All those storyboard scenes that you implemented using the screen navigation patterns in Chapter 3 were intentionally simple. Obviously, a useful mobile app provides rich content and offers better functionality to gracefully interact with users. The user interface (UI) will certainly play an important role in the overall user experience.

The techniques and vocabularies for creating meaningful user interfaces for iOS are definitely different from those for most of the front-end and back-end web development platforms. UI components are normally platform dependent. You just need to know the application programming interface (API) usages of the user interface widgets and where to look up the platform-specific widget specifications.

iOS content views and storyboard scenes are structured in a view container (view-parent) model, which has existed in the industry for a long time. In iOS, UIView is an object that draws content and UI widgets on the screen with which the user can interact. A UIView is also a container that holds other UIView objects to define the hierarchical layout of the UI.

To position UI widgets in the content view, iOS uses Auto Layout to set the location and size of the widgets within each one's parent view or relative to a sibling.

> **Note**   There might be some similarities between the iOS UI framework and HTML mock-up structures. However, I think the amount of similarity is not enough to help you to understand the iOS UIKit framework. I strongly suggest you have an open mind and learn the object-oriented style of the iOS UI framework from scratch without trying to force your current HTML and web approaches into this subject.

UIView

The UIView object is the basic building block for UI components. It is the base class for all widgets, such as common widgets like UIButton and UILabel. It is also used as the parent container view.

WEB ANALOGY

In HTML, there is no equivalent for a UI base class, but an HTML element like <div> has few default attributes but its look and behavior can be customized in infinite ways.

A visible UIView occupies a rectangular area on the screen and is responsible for drawing and event handling. The UIViewController class has a root view defined in the UIViewController.view property that is inherited by all the view controllers. All UI widgets are special types of the UIView object that have attributes for the intended look and feel and behaviors. When drawing the view elements in a storyboard, they are added to the parent view, and you use the storyboard view inspectors to visually edit the view properties.

All the iOS UI widgets inherit from UIView. You can set the inherited UIView attributes in the storyboard view's Attributes Inspector. For example, Figure 4-1 depicts the View section in the Attributes Inspector for UI widgets.

Figure 4-1. View section of the Attributes Inspector

At runtime, you can programmatically update the properties of the UIView object. UIView is the ultimate superclass of all widgets. It offers a fairly rich API for developers to implement a number of UI-related responsibilities, such as the following:

- Rendering content
- Layout and manage subviews
- Event handling
- Animations

The rest of the chapter demonstrates the common attributes or APIs that you most likely will encounter or that are just good to know now. Before diving into common iOS UI widgets from the iOS software development kit

(SDK), I will talk about an important related topic, application resources, which are used by the UI widgets as well as many other common programming tasks.

Application Resources

Most GUI apps are composed of more than programming code; they require other resources, such as images and externalized strings. In iOS, you will encounter similar tasks for how to provide different assets for different device configurations. This section will demonstrate how to implement two common use cases in Xcode: using the assets catalog and externalizing strings.

Using the Assets Catalog

You can group images for different device configurations in the *assets catalog*. This simplifies the management of the images for different screen sizes and device configurations when using them in your iOS code. This section will show you how to do this in iOS. Do the following:

1. Launch Xcode, use the Single View Application template, and name the project **CommonWidgets**. The project comes with one assets catalog, Images.xcassets, that already contains the AppIcon set, as shown in Figure 4-2 (left pointer). The editor shows you the icons and pixel resolutions for different device types. Toggle the iOS 6.1 and Prior Sizes check box (right pointer in Figure 4-2) to see the differences in the editor.

Figure 4-2. AppIcon set in Images.xcassets

2. Create images for the iOS app icon with the different image resolutions specified in the editor. Drag the appropriate image files to the guided squares. Figure 4-3 depicts the result.

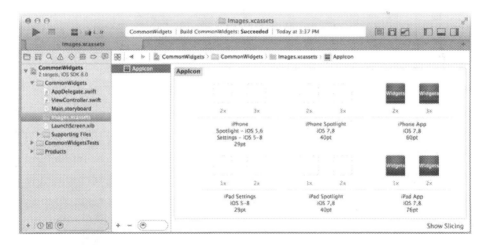

Figure 4-3. Re-creating icons for iOS with Images.xcassets

3. To add a regular image asset, click the Add (+) button and select New Image Set, as shown in Figure 4-4.

    a. Use the Attributes Inspector to select the type of devices you want to provide.

    b. You can choose to supply the image set by selecting the Universal size class or other device-specific types. Either way, 1x, 2x, and 3x should cover all the iOS devices now.

    c. Select the image with 1x resolution and drag it to the right spot (as shown by the pointer under the sample in Figure 4-4). Repeat the step for the 2x and 3x images.

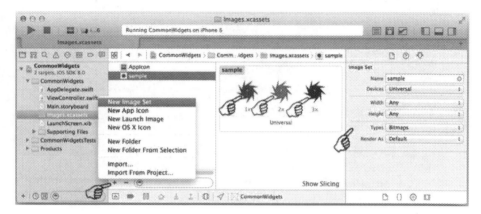

Figure 4-4. Adding an image set in Images.xcassets

    d. Give the image set a name (for example, type **sample**). The name is the identifier to access the image from your code or from a storyboard.

You have created two image assets. The first, AppIcon, is used for the launch icon on the home screen by default. The other one, sample, can be used by your code or any widgets in your storyboard. You will use the sample icon in later exercises.

> **Note** You can use your favorite image editor to create the images or download them from www.pdachoice.com/bookassets.

Externalizing Strings

Generally, you store string text in external files. Both Android and iOS read externalized strings in a similar manner. In iOS, they are stored in "key" = "value"; format in .strings files. In your Swift code, instead of hard-coding the values directly, use the system API to get the string values by key. This is similar to the method for localizing web applications for international audiences. To externalize strings for an iOS project, do the following:

1. Create a new file anywhere in your Xcode project. For example, to create a new file in the Supporting Files folder, press ⌘+N (the keyboard shortcut for New File).

    a. On the "Choose a template" screen, select iOS ➤ Resource ➤ Strings File.

    b. Save the file as Localizable.strings. This is the default file name used by the iOS API. You can create multiple .strings files and specify the file name using the iOS system API.

2. Copy Listing 4-1 into your iOS Localizable.strings to start with. You will use these strings later.

Listing 4-1. iOS Localizable.strings

```
"app_name" = "HelloAndroid";
"action_settings" = "Settings";
"hello_world" = "Hello world!";
"hello_button" = "Hello ...";
"name_hint" = "Enter a Name, i.e, You";
```

3. To read the strings from the Localizable.strings file, use the NSLocalizedString(...) method to retrieve the string by key, as shown in Listing 4-2.

Listing 4-2. Read Strings from the iOS Localizable.strings File

```
// hello_world" = "Hello world!";
var str = NSLocalizedString("hello_world", comment: "")
println(str) // Hello world!
```

With the strings externalized in a text file, you can translate the text to different languages, a common process to implement internationalization. Although I will not cover localization/internationalization in depth, the concept and process are similar in many programming platforms.

Common UI Widgets

UI widgets are the interactive software-control components in the application's UI, such as buttons, text fields, and so forth. You create screens to contain the appropriate UI widgets to interact with users, to collect information from users, and to display information to users.

The iOS UIKit framework provides rich system UI widgets that you "draw" in the storyboard. You also "connect" them to the Swift class as IBOutlet properties so that your code can directly use the view object, update its attributes, or invoke the widget methods to provide dynamic application behaviors.

The rest of this section introduces the common iOS UI widgets and compares them with web UI components when appropriate. Continuing with the CommonWidgets project created previously, do the following:

1. The storyboard already has a storyboard scene that pairs with the ViewController class. This scene won't be tall enough for all the widgets you're going to add. Just to enable you to see all the widgets to be added to this scene, change the Simulated Metrics size to Freeform and make it long enough so you can see all the widgets in storyboard.

2. Select the View Controller from the storyboard, and in the Size Inspector, change Simulated Size to Freeform. Make the size 320x1500 (Figure 4-5) to give the view enough height to start with.

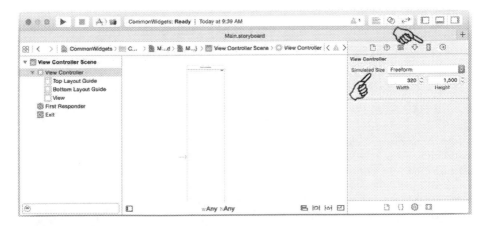

Figure 4-5. Changing the simulated size in the storyboard to Freeform

Later, you will wrap the whole screen in a scroll view so that you can scroll the view up and down.

> **Note**   Don't bother implementing Auto Layout for each widget in the beginning. The Auto Layout constraints will get messed up while setting up `UIScrollView`. Instead, implement the Auto Layout constraints after you set up the scroll view.

UILabel

WEB ANALOGY

`<h1>` to `<h6>` or `<p>` elements are commonly used in HTML pages.

You commonly use `UILabel` to draw one or multiple lines of static text, such as those that identify other parts of your UI.

Using the Android app as the wireframe, add a `UILabel` to the iOS CommonWidgets app by following these steps:

1. Select `Main.storyboard` and drag a `Label` from the Object Library to the root view, as shown in Figure 4-6. Drag the widget to position the `UILabel`, as shown in the Size Inspector.

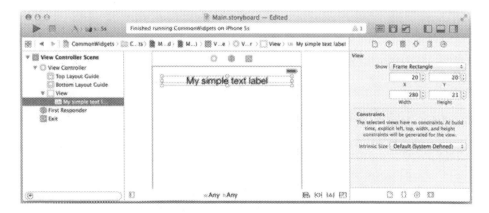

Figure 4-6. Adjusting UILabel size and position

2. Update the `UILabel` attributes in the Attributes Inspector, as shown in Figure 4-7.

    a. For Text, enter **My simple text label**.

    b. *For* Alignment, use center alignment.

    c. The other options (Shadow, Autoshrink, and so on) are all safe to play with, too.

Figure 4-7. Updating UILabel attributes

3. Open the Assistant Editor and connect `IBOutlet` in the Connections Inspector to your code so that you can update `UILabel` programmatically. Most of the attributes in the Attributes Inspector can be modified in the runtime via the `IBOutlet mLabel` property, as shown in Listing 4-3.

Listing 4-3. UILabel Properties

```
...
@IBOutlet weak var mLabel: UILabel!
override func viewDidLoad() {
  super.viewDidLoad()
  // Do any additional setup after loading the view ...
  self.initLabel()
}

func initLabel() {
  self.mLabel.text = "My simple text label"
  self.mLabel.textColor = UIColor.darkTextColor()
  self.mLabel.textAlignment = NSTextAlignment.Center
  self.mLabel.shadowColor = UIColor.lightGrayColor()
  self.mLabel.shadowOffset = CGSize(width: 2, height: -2)
}
...
```

Build and run the CommonWidgets app to see the UILabel in action
(Figure 4-8).

Figure 4-8. A simple iOS UILabel look and feel

UITextField

```
                          WEB ANALOGY
```

<input> elements are commonly used in HTML pages.

In iOS, UITextField accepts a single line of user input and shows placeholder text when the user input is still empty. To learn by example, do the following to use UITextField in the CommonWidgets project:

1. Select Main.storyboard and drag a TextField from the Object Library to the root view, as shown in Figure 4-9. Position the UITextField right under the UILabel.

Figure 4-9. Changing the UITextField size and position

2. Update its attributes in the Attributes Inspector as shown in Figure 4-10.

    a. For Placeholder, enter "Hint: one-line text input."

    b. Fill in the other attributes as shown in Figure 4-10.

Figure 4-10. Defining UITextField in the Attributes Inspector

3. Open the Assistant Editor and connect the following
    outlets in the Connections Inspector to your code, as
    shown in Listing 4-4:

    a. Connect IBOutlet to the mTextField property so that you
        can update UITextField programmatically.

    b. Connect the delegate outlet to the ViewController class
        so that the UITextField sends a message to its
        delegate object.

    c. Implement the UITextFieldDelegate protocol in
        ViewController. Listing 4-4 shows the common way to
        dismiss the keyboard when the Return key is pressed.

> **Note**   Other methods are defined in UITextFieldDelegate. ⌘-click
> the symbol in the editor to bring up the class definition. I normally check
> the method signatures without memorizing them.

Listing 4-4. UITextFieldDelegate

```
class ViewController: UIViewController, UITextFieldDelegate {
  ...
  @IBOutlet weak var mTextField: UITextField!

  // called when 'return' key pressed. return false to ignore.
  func textFieldShouldReturn(textField: UITextField!) -> Bool {
    textField.resignFirstResponder()
    return true
  }
  ...
```

Build and run the CommonWidgets app to see UITextField in action.

UITextView

WEB ANALOGY

<textarea> elements are commonly used in HTML pages.

In iOS, UITextView accepts and displays multiple lines of text. To learn by
example, do the following to use UITextView in the CommonWidgets project:

1. Select Main.storyboard and drag a UITextView
    from the Object Library to the root view, as shown
    in Figure 4-11. Position the widget right under the
    UITextField.

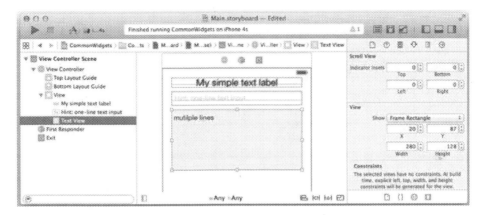

Figure 4-11. Changing the UITextView size and position

2. Update its attributes in the Attributes Inspector:

    a. For Text, enter "multiple lines."

    b. Take a look at its Attributes Inspector. Many attributes are
        similar to the UITextField but not exactly (for example, there
        is no Placeholder attribute).

3. Open the Assistant Editor and connect IBOutlet in
    the Connections Inspector to your code, mTextView,
    so that you can update UITextView programmatically.
    Add a method, logText(...), that prints text to
    UITextView. You will use it later (see Listing 4-5).

Listing 4-5. UITextView Properties

```
class ViewController: UIViewController ... {
  ...
  @IBOutlet weak var mTextView: UITextView!
  func logText(text : String) {
    self.mTextView.text = self.mTextView.text + "\n" + text

    // to make sure the last line is visible
    var count = self.mTextView.text.utf16Count // string length
    self.mTextView.scrollRangeToVisible(NSMakeRange(count, 0))
  }
  ...
```

UITextView can have multiple lines separated by line breaks. You won't be able to dismiss the keyboard the same way you normally do for UITextField. Normally, you use another control; for instance, if you have a save button, you may use it to trigger View.resignFirstResponder() to dismiss the keyboard.

UIButton

```
ANDROID ANALOGY
```

<button> or <input type="button"> form elements are commonly used in HTML pages.

In iOS, UIButton, the common Button control widget, intercepts touch events and sends an action message to the delegate. To learn by example, do the following in the CommonWidgets project:

1. Select Main.storyboard, drag a UIButton from the Object Library to the root view, and position the UIButton right under the text view, as shown in Figure 4-12.

2. Update its attributes in the Attributes Inspector (see Figure 4-12).

    a. Most of the Button attributes are associated with the button states. Set the State Config attribute first to Default.

    b. Set Title to Action Button.

    c. Set Image to sample.

    d. The other settings are all safe to play with. You may accept the defaults, as shown in Figure 4-12.

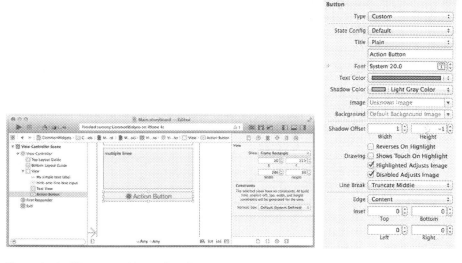

Figure 4-12. UIButton position and attributes

3.   Open the Assistant Editor and connect IBOutlet and
     IBAction in the Connections Inspector to your code,
     as shown in Listing 4-6.

Listing 4-6. IBOutlet and Implement IBAction

```
class ViewController: UIViewController, UITextFieldDelegate {
  ...
  @IBOutlet weak var mButton: UIButton!
  @IBAction func doButtonTouchDown(sender: AnyObject) {
    println(self.mButton.titleForState(UIControlState.Normal))
    self.mButton.setTitle("Click me!", forState: UIControlState.Normal)
    self.logText("Button clicked")
  }
  ...
```

Build and run the CommonWidgets app to make sure everything is good.
When the button is clicked, it simply logs the "Button clicked" text in the
UITextView (see Figure 4-13).

Figure 4-13. Button clicked in UITextView

UISegmentedControl

In iOS, `UISegmentedControl` offers closely related but mutually exclusive choices. To show and learn by example, do the following in the CommonWidgets app:

1. Select `Main.storyboard` and drag a `UISegmentedControl` from the Object Library to the root view under the button, as shown in Figure 4-14.

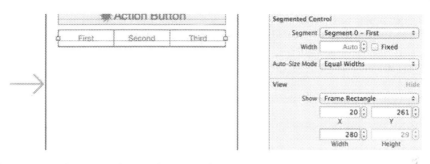

Figure 4-14. UISegmentedControl size and position

2. Update its attribute in the Attributes Inspector
    (see Figure 4-15):

    a. For Style, select Bar.

    b. Set Segments to 3.

    c. For Title, select First, Second, and Third for each segment,
        respectfully.

    d. Optionally, you may assign an image instead of title for
        each segment.

    e. You can check the Selected segment
        (for example, Segment 0).

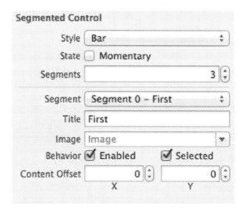

Figure 4-15. UISegmentedControl attributes

3. Open the Assistant Editor and connect `IBOutlet`
    and `IBAction` in the Connections Inspector to your
    code. Frequently, you implement `IBAction` for the
    Value Changed events to capture the selections
    (see Listing 4-7).

Listing 4-7. UISegmentControl IBOutlet and Implement IBAction

```
class ViewController: ...{
  ...
  @IBOutlet weak var mSegmentedControl: UISegmentedControl!
  @IBAction func doScValueChanged(sender: AnyObject) {
    var idx = self.mSegmentedControl.selectedSegmentIndex
    self.logText("segment \(idx)")
  }
  ...
```

Build and run the CommonWidgets app to see `UISegmentedControl` in
action. Each segment has a zero-based index (see Figure 4-16).

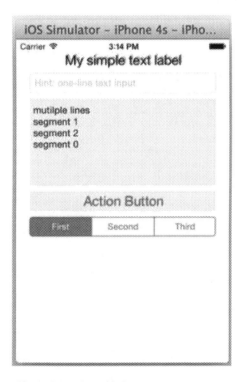

Figure 4-16. UISegmentedControl zero-based index

UISlider

WEB ANALOGY

`<input type="range">` elements are commonly used in HTML pages.

---

iOS's `UISlider` allows users to make adjustments to a value given a range of allowed values. Users drag the slider left or right to set the value. The interactive nature of the slider makes it a great choice for settings that reflect intensity levels, such as volume, brightness, or color saturation.

To demonstrate the iOS `UISlider`, do the following:

1. Select `Main.storyboard`, drag a `UISlider` from the Object Library, and place it below the `UISegmentedControl` object, as shown in Figure 4-17.

2. Update its attributes in the Attributes Inspector (see Figure 4-17):

    a. Set the Min value to 0 and the max to 100.

    b. Min Image and Max Image.

    c. Leave Min Track Tint and Max Track Tint at the defaults.

    d. Disable Continuous Updates.

Figure 4-17. Updating the UISlider attributes

3. Open the Assistant Editor and connect `IBOutlet` and `IBAction` to your code in the Connections Inspector. You will often implement `IBAction` for the Value Changed event to capture the selections (see Listing 4-8).

Listing 4-8. UISlider IBOutlet and Implement IBAction

```
class ViewController: ...{
  ...
  @IBOutlet weak var mSlider: UISlider!
  @IBAction func doSliderValueChanged(sender: AnyObject) {
    var value = self.mSlider.value
    self.logText("slider: \(value)")
  }
  ...
```

Build and run the CommonWidgets app to see UISlider in action. As you move the slider by dragging the circle on the slider, called thumb, its value continues to be printed in the UITextView (see Figure 4-18).

Figure 4-18. UISlider value updates

UIActivityIndicatorView

WEB ANALOGY

This is not a built-in HTML element, but it is commonly implemented in front-end web pages using JavaScript or CSS.

UIActivityIndicatorView displays a "busy" activity indicator for a task or something else in progress. You may commonly call it a spinner, loader, or wait cursor in your web app. To learn and visualize this iOS UI widget, do the following in the CommonWidgets iOS app:

1. Select Main.storyboard, drag a UIActivityIndicatorView from the Object Library, and position it left-aligned and below the UISlider (see Figure 4-19).

2. Update its attribute in the Attributes Inspector, as shown in Figure 4-19:

    a. *Style*: Set this to Gray.

    b. *Color*: Set this to Default.

    c. *Behavior*: Both Animating and Hides When Stopped are commonly enabled.

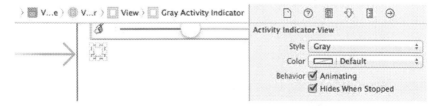

Figure 4-19. UIActivityIndicatorView attributes

3. Open the Assistant Editor and connect IBOutlet in the Connections Inspector to your code so that you can enable or disable the activity indicator, as shown in Listing 4-9.

Listing 4-9. UIActivityIndicatorView IBOutlet

```
class ViewController: ...{
  ...
  @IBOutlet weak var mActivityIndicator: UIActivityIndicatorView!
  func toggleActivityIndicator() {
    var isAnimating = mActivityIndicator.isAnimating()
    isAnimating ? mActivityIndicator.stopAnimating() : mActivityIndicator.
    startAnimating()
  }
  ...
```

Build and run the CommonWidgets app to see the iOS animated activity indicator. You will call the `toggleActivityIndicator()` method later.

UIProgressView

ANDROID ANALOGY

HTML `<progress>` elements (new in HTML 5) are commonly used in HTML pages.

To show a task with a known duration in progress, use `UIProgressView` to show how far the task has progressed. With this, users can better anticipate how much longer until it completes. To learn and visualize how the iOS `UIProgressView` works, do the following:

1. Select `Main.storyboard`, drag a `UIProgressView` from the Object Library, and position it below and left-aligned to the activity indicator, as shown in Figure 4-20.

2. Update its attributes in the Attributes Inspector (see Figure 4-20).

   a. *Style*: Default (or Bar)

   b. *Progress*: 0.5 (between 0.0 and 1.0)

   c. *Progress Tint*: Purple

   d. *Track Tint*: Yellow

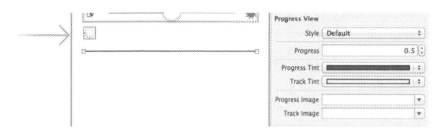

Figure 4-20. *UIActivityIndicatorView attributes*

3. Open the Assistant Editor and connect IBOutlet in the
    Connections Inspector to your code so that you can
    update UIProgressView programmatically. Modify the
    UISlider delegate method, doSliderValueChanged(...)
    as shown in Listing 4-10.

Listing 4-10. *UIActivityIndicatorView IBOutlet*

```
class ViewController: ...{
  ...
  @IBAction func doSliderValueChanged(sender: AnyObject) {
    ...
    self.updateProgress(value/100)
  }
  ...
  @IBOutlet weak var mProgressView: UIProgressView!
  func updateProgress(value: Float) {
    self.mProgressView.progress = value
  }
  ...
```

Build and run the CommonWidgets app to visualize iOS's UIProgressView in
action (see Figure 4-21).

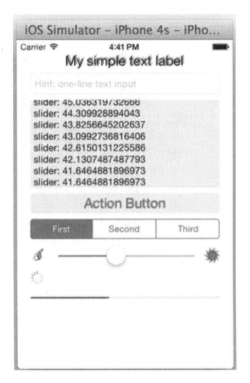

Figure 4-21. UIProgressView update in action

UISwitch

```
                    WEB ANALOGY
```

<input type="checkbox"> elements are commonly used in HTML pages.

The switch-like widgets are user friendly for presenting mutually exclusive choices. In web pages, you may find widgets with many different styles for the same purpose. In iOS, you use UISwitch to allow a user to change values by toggling or dragging the thumb between two states.

To learn UISwitch by example, do the following:

1.   Select Main.storyboard and drag a UISwitch
      from the Object Library. Position it to the right of
      UIActivityIndicatorView (see Figure 4-22).

2. Update its attribute in the Attributes Inspector (see Figure 4-22).

    a. Set State to On.

    b. You can change any other attributes safely.

Figure 4-22. UIActivityIndicatorView

3. Open the Assistant Editor and connect IBOutlet and IBAction in the Connections Inspector to your code. You will often implement IBAction for the Value Changed event to capture the selections (see Listing 4-11).

Listing 4-11. UISwitch IBOutlet

```
class ViewController: ...{
  ...
  @IBOutlet var mSwitch: UISwitch!
  @IBAction func doSwitchValueChanged(sender: AnyObject) {
    var isOn = self.mSwitch.on
    self.toggleActivityIndicator()
  }
  ...
```

Build and run the app and toggle the UISwitch to see the activity indicator's animation changes (see Figure 4-23).

Figure 4-23. iOS UISwitch look and feel

UIImageView

WEB ANALOGY

HTML `<img>` elements are commonly used in HTML pages.

In iOS, `UIImageView` displays one image or a series of images for simple graphic animations. For a simple usage like the CommonWidgets app, all you need to do is specify the image source and the attributes in a storyboard for how you want to render the image.

To learn iOS `UIImageView` by example, do the following:

1. `UIImageView` can now render vector-based images! This is a new feature in Xcode 6. I only know that the first page of a PDF is rendered nicely. You can definitely use a bitmap image for this exercise or create a new image set for a PDF file, as shown by the pointers in Figure 4-24.

   a. Select `Images.xcassets` to add a new image set. Name it `pdf`.

   b. In `pdf`, set Type to Vectors in the Attributes Inspector.

   c. Drag a PDF file to the universal slot, as shown in Figure 4-22. There is no need to provide 2x or 3x images.

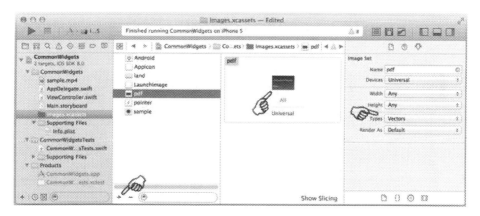

Figure 4-24. Creating an image set

2. Select `Main.storyboard`, drag a `UIImageView` object from the Object Library to the view, and position it under the `UIProgressView` object, as shown in Figure 4-25.

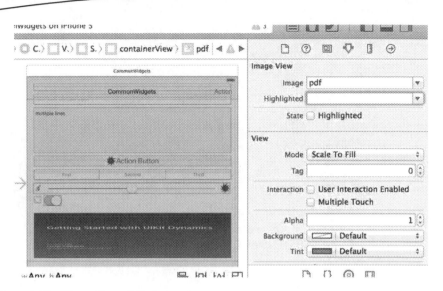

Figure 4-25. UIImageView attributes

3. Update its attributes in the Attributes Inspector:

    a. Set Image to pdf.

    b. Set Mode to Aspect Fit.

    c. Set the others as shown in Figure 4-23.

4. Open the Assistant Editor and connect IBOutlet in the Connections Inspector to your code. Listing 4-12 demonstrates a simple setImage(...) method that assigns an UIImage object to UIImageView.

Listing 4-12. UISwitch IBOutlet

```
class ViewController: ...{
  ...
  @IBOutlet weak var mImageView: UIImageView!
  func setImage(name: String) {
    self.mImageView.image = UIImage(named: name)
  }
  ...
```

As you can see in Figure 4-25, there are few attributes you need to master. However, when it comes to creating a UIImage and optimizing its size and performance, you want to look into the UIImage class to see how you would construct the UIImage instance from various sources. There are actually iOS frameworks that primarily deal with images, like Quartz 2D or OpenGL.

If you know **WebGL**, you definitely want to take advantage of your existing knowledge and explore the counterpart iOS OpenGL framework. If you come from a graphics-editing background, Quartz 2D offers a rich graphics API that will support you for iOS graphics-editing tasks.

You can build and run the CommonWidgets iOS app to see UIImageView in action, as shown in Figure 4-26.

Figure 4-26. UIImageView in iPhone 5

Menu

Menus are used to provide quick access to frequently used actions. They are particularly common in desktop, Android, and web apps. Although there is no such similarly named feature in the iOS SDK, UIBarButtonItem in UIToolbar or UINavigationBar serves a similar purpose: quick access.

UIBarButtonItem

WEB ANALOGY

This is usually implemented with an add-on UI widget library.

For quick access actions in iOS, you commonly use `UIBarButtonItem` in the navigation bar for a limited number of action buttons that can fit into the fixed space. On the iPhone, you can create a bottom bar, `UIToolbar`, if all of the buttons in `UIBarButtonItem` don't fit on the top navigation bar.

To learn and show the `UIBarButtonItem` in the navigation bar and toolbar by example, do the following in the CommonWidgets project:

1. Drag a `UINavigationBar` from the Object Library to the `view` and position it on top of the view. Frequently, you will just select the View Controller to embed it in a `NavigationController` in the storyboard (from the Xcode menu bar, select Editor ➤ Embed In ➤ Navigation Controller). Figure 4-27 depicts the operation results in a new Navigation Controller scene and a Navigation Item in the existing View Controller scene:

    a. Multiselect all the widgets in the scene and reposition them to make room for the top bar.

    b. Update the Navigation Item attributes in the Attributes Inspector (for example, enter **CommonWidgets** for Title).

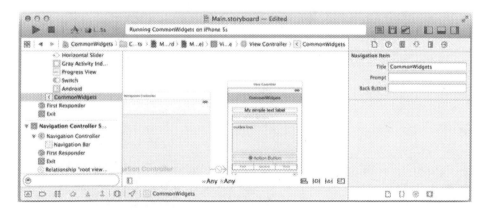

Figure 4-27. Navigation Controller and Navigation Bar

2. Double-click the Navigation Bar to select it and drag a `UIBarButtonItem` from the Object Library onto the right side of the Navigation Bar to add a `rightBarButtonItem` (see Figure 4-28). Choose an `Identifier` from selections for those common actions. Or enter a title, such as **Action**, as shown in Figure 4-28.

Figure 4-28. *UIBarButtonItem attributes*

3. Open the Assistant Editor and connect `IBAction` in the `UIBarButtonItem` Connections Inspector to your code (see Listing 4-13).

Listing 4-13. *UIBarButtonItem IBOutlet and IBAction*

```
class ViewController: ...{
  ...
  @IBAction func doBarButtonAction(sender: AnyObject) {
    println(">> doBarButtonAction")
  }
  ...
```

Action Sheet

WEB ANALOGY

This is an add-on modal window widget.

In web apps, you can use a modal callout to prompt users to make a selection. The operations and the look and feel (L&F) establish a strong relationship to the context that originates the operations. On the iPad, you can safely choose `UIPopoverController` (see Chapter 3) to present the list of selections, which on the iPhone is automatically presented full-screen.

If you don't want to use full-screen, perhaps for a smaller selection you can choose UIActionSheet, which is presented as a pop-over for the iPad or in an sheet that emerges from the bottom of the screen for smaller iPhone devices.

The key SDK class is UIAlertController, which was introduced in Chapter 3 for alert dialogs (see Listing 3-22). To learn the iOS UIActionSheet by example, modify the previous doBarButtonAction(...) IBAction method as shown in Listing 4-14.

1. Create an instance of UIAlertController with the style UIAlertControllerStyle.ActionSheet.

2. You can use Title or Message to establish a visual connection to the originating context.

3. It is common to have a destructive UIAlertAction in red for a delete or remove action, which is specified with the UIAlertActionStyle.Destructive style.

4. UIActionSheet is presented as a pop-over on the iPad. You need to specify location information or the barButtonItem.

Listing 4-14. UIAlertController with ActionSheet Style

```
class ViewController: ...{
  ...
  @IBAction func doBarButtonAction(sender: AnyObject) {
    println(">> doBarButtonDone: ")

    var actionSheet = UIAlertController(title: "Action (from bar
    button item)", message: "Choose an Action", preferredStyle:
    UIAlertControllerStyle.ActionSheet)

    // add action buttons
    var actionCancel = UIAlertAction(title: "Cancel", style:
    UIAlertActionStyle.Cancel,
      handler: {action in
      // do nothing
      })

    var actionNormal1 = UIAlertAction(title: "Action 1", style:
    UIAlertActionStyle.Default,
      handler: {action in
        println(">> actionNormal1")
      })
```

```
var actionNormal2 = UIAlertAction(title: "Action 2", style:
UIAlertActionStyle.Default,
  handler: {action in
    println(">> actionNormal2")
  })

var actionDestruct = UIAlertAction(title: "Destruct", style:
UIAlertActionStyle.Destructive,
  handler: {action in
    println(">> actionDestruct")
  })

actionSheet.addAction(actionCancel) // always the last one
actionSheet.addAction(actionNormal1)
actionSheet.addAction(actionNormal2)
actionSheet.addAction(actionDestruct)

// UIViewController API to presend viewController
// 4. for iPAD support
if let popoverController = actionSheet.popoverPresentationController {
  popoverController.barButtonItem = sender as UIBarButtonItem
}

self.presentViewController(actionSheet, animated: true, completion: nil)
}
...
```

Build and run the CommonWidgets app to visualize the iOS UIActionSheet
(see Figure 4-29).

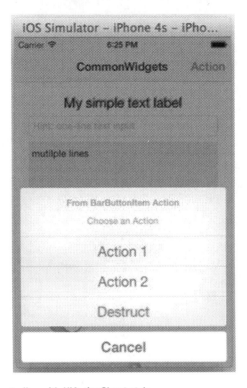

Figure 4-29. UIAlertController with UIActionSheet style

UIPickerView

WEB ANALOGY

HTML <select> elements are commonly used in HTML pages.

In iOS, UIPickerView displays a set of values from which the user selects. It provides a quick way to select one value from a spinning wheel–like list that shows all or part of the selections.

In traditional desktop apps or web pages, you normally see a drop-down list for this purpose, except with one trivial difference: drop-downs show only the selected value while the other choices are not shown after selected.

The iOS `UIPickerView` uses the same pattern as `UITableView` `DataSource` to supply the items. To learn by example, add a `UIPickerView` widget to the CommonWidgets app and do the following:

1. Select `Main.storyboard` and drag a `UIPickerView` from the Object Library. Position it below the `UIImageView` (see Figure 4-30).

Figure 4-30. Placing the UIPickerView

2. Open the Assistant Editor and establish `UIPickerView` outlet connections to your code in the Connections Inspector (see Figure 4-31).

    a. Connect `IBOutlet` to your code.

    b. Connect the `delegate` and `dataSource` outlets to the `ViewController` class (just like `UITableView` or any widgets using `data source`).

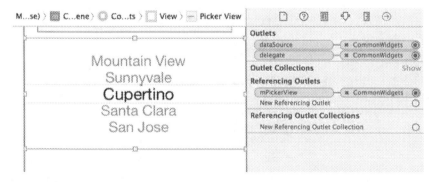

Figure 4-31. Connecting the UIPickerView outlets

3.   To implement the `UIPickerView` delegate and
     data source, declare the `ViewController` class
     to implement the `UIPickerViewDelegate` and
     `UIPickerViewDataSource` protocols, as shown in
     Listing 4-15.

Listing 4-15. UIPickerView IBOutlet

```
class ViewController: ... , UIPickerViewDelegate, UIPickerViewDataSource {
  ...
  @IBOutlet weak var mPickerView: UIPickerView!
  // returns the number of 'columns' to display.
  func numberOfComponentsInPickerView(pickerView: UIPickerView) -> Int {
    return 2
  }

  // returns the # of rows in each component..
  func pickerView(pickerView: UIPickerView, numberOfRowsInComponent
  component: Int) -> Int {
    return 10
  }

  func pickerView(pickerView: UIPickerView, titleForRow row: Int,
  forComponent component: Int) -> String! {
    return "(\(component), \(row))"
  }

  func pickerView(pickerView: UIPickerView, didSelectRow row: Int,
  inComponent component: Int) {
    println("\(self.mPickerView.selectedRowInComponent(0))")
    // before selection
    println("\(self.mPickerView.selectedRowInComponent(1))")
    println("(\(component), \(row))") // current selection
  }
  ...
```

Build and run the app to see iOS's `UIPickerView` in action. The iPhone
emulator is too small for all the widgets you have so far. You need a
browser-like `scroll bar` (which you will implement soon). You can run it in
the iPad emulator for now (see Figure 4-32).

Figure 4-32. UIPickerView in the iPad emulator

Note that if the app looks like a big iPhone while running in the iPad emulator and all the widgets simply scale up, your project deployment information must have been set to iPhone only. Change the deployment device to Universal under Deployment Info, as shown by the pointer in Figure 4-33.

Figure 4-33. Changing Devices to Universal in Deployment Info

Play Video

The iOS SDK gives you an easy-to-use API to play video resources from a URL. To play full-screen video, you can use the `MPMoviePlayerViewController` class, which already has the appropriate content view and media player controls built in. You only need to present the whole view controller. The following steps (see Listing 4-16) demonstrate the simplest usage:

1. Implement the `useMoviePlayerViewController()` method, which plays a video in `MPMoviePlayerViewController` (see Listing 4-16).

    a. Create an instance with a URL link to a remote video source. iOS supports the HTTP Live Streaming (HLS) protocol. You can also create a file URL for bundled content, as shown in the commented code in Listing 4-16. Just as you would in web apps, make sure the video format is supported. MPEG4 QuickTime is fairly agnostic, and HLS is good for progressive loading.

    b. `MPMoviePlayerViewController` contains a `MPMoviePlayerController` property, which is the core class to play video. Almost all the customization is done via this property. You will use this class in a moment.

2. Earlier you implemented two actions in an UIActionSheet (see Figure 4-29). Use the Action 1 button to trigger the `useMoviePlayerViewController()` method (see Listing 4-16).

Listing 4-16. useMoviePlayerViewController()

```
import MediaPlayer
...
class ViewController: ...{
   ...
   @IBAction func doBarButtonAction(sender: AnyObject) {
     ...
     var actionNormal1 = UIAlertAction(title: "Action 1", style:
```

```
UIAlertActionStyle.Default,
    handler: {action in
      println(">> actionNormal1")
      self.useMpMoviePlayerViewController()
    })
  ...
}
...
func useMpMoviePlayerViewController() {
//   var filepath = NSBundle.mainBundle().
     pathForResource("sample.mp4", ofType: nil)
//   var fileUrl = NSURL(fileURLWithPath: filepath)
//   var pvc = MPMoviePlayerViewController(contentURL: fileUrl)

  var contentUrl = NSURL(string: "http://devimages.apple.com/
  iphone/samples/bipbop/gear3/prog_index.m3u8")
  var pvc = MPMoviePlayerViewController(contentURL: contentUrl)

  pvc.moviePlayer.shouldAutoplay = false;
  pvc.moviePlayer.repeatMode = MPMovieRepeatMode.One

  self.presentViewController(pvc, animated: true, completion: nil)
}
...
```

3. To play video in non-full-screen mode, use
    MPMoviePlayerController directly to play video in a
    UIView widget:

    a. Select Main.storyboard, drag a UIView from the Object
        Library, and position it below the UIPickerView, as shown in
        Figure 4-34. This is the viewing area that shows the video.

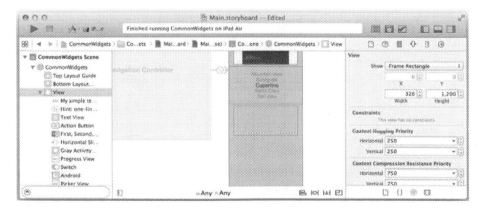

Figure 4-34. View element for the video

b. Open the Assistant Editor to connect IBOutlet in the Connections Inspector to your code's mVideoView property.

c. Create a stored property for the MPMoviePlayerController instance to allow users to seek through, play, or stop the playback.

d. In viewDidLoad(...), invoke the useMoviePlayerController() method to prepare the video to play.

e. Use the Action 2 button to start the video (see Listing 4-17).

Listing 4-17. Using the MPMoviePlayercontroller

```
class ViewController: ...{
  ...
  override func viewDidLoad() {
    ...
    self.useMoviePlayerController()
  }
  ...
  @IBOutlet weak var mVideoView: UIView!
  var mMoviePlayer : MPMoviePlayerController!
  func useMoviePlayerController() {
    var url = NSURL(string: "http://devimages.apple.com/iphone/samples/
    bipbop/gear3/prog_index.m3u8")
    self.mMoviePlayer = MPMoviePlayerController(contentURL: url)

    self.mMoviePlayer.shouldAutoplay = false
    self.mMoviePlayer.controlStyle = MPMovieControlStyle.Embedded
    self.mMoviePlayer.setFullscreen(false, animated: true)

    self.mMoviePlayer.view.frame = self.mVideoView.bounds
    self.mVideoView.addSubview(self.mMoviePlayer.view)

    self.mMoviePlayer.currentPlaybackTime = 2.0
    self.mMoviePlayer.prepareToPlay()
  }
  ...
  @IBAction func doBarButtonAction(sender: AnyObject) {
    ...
    var actionNormal2 = UIAlertAction(title: "Action 2", style:
    UIAlertActionStyle.Default,
      handler: {action in
        self.mMoviePlayer.play()
      })
    ...
}
```

Build and run the app. Select Action 1 for full-screen and Action 2 to play video embedded in a subview. You don't have the browser-like scroll view yet, but you can run it in the iPad emulator for now (see Figure 4-35).

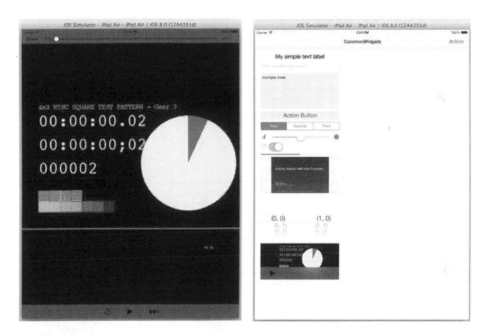

Figure 4-35. Playing video full-screen vs. embedded in the iPad emulator

UIWebView

WEB ANALOGY

HTML <iframe> elements are commonly used in HTML pages..

You can display rich HTML content in your mobile apps on almost all the popular mobile platforms, including iOS, Android, BlackBerry, and Windows phones. This enables you to deliver web content as part of your mobile apps. One common scenario is when you want to provide information in your app that needs to be updated frequently and you want to host the content online as a web page. To take it one step further, the web content does not have to be remote; you can bundle the web page content with the native app. This enables web developers to leverage their web development skills and create so-called hybrid apps.

With new features from HTML5 and CSS3, many web developers are creating meaningful and interactive web apps that are shortening the gap between native apps and mobile web apps. In iOS, the key SDK class is UIWebView, and it supports many HTML5 and CSS3 features (for example, offline cache and web sockets, and so on).

As an example, the following steps demonstrate common tasks using UIWebView:

1. Select Main.storyboard, drag a UIWebView from the Object Library, and position it below the video View (see Figure 4-36). Set its attributes in the Attributes Inspector; it is commonly set to Scales Page To Fit.

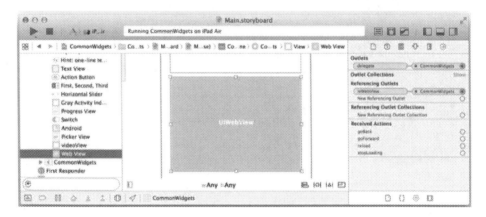

Figure 4-36. iOS UIWebView delegate in the Connections Inspector

2. As usual, open the Assistant Editor and connect the following outlets in the Connections Inspector to your code (see Figure 4-36):

    a. Connect IBOutlet so you can use the widget in your code.

    b. Connect the delegate outlet so your code can intercept UIWebView life-cycle events.

3. Listing 4-18 demonstrates the programming code commonly used for UIWebView.

    a. Use loadRequest(...) to load the URL. You can also create a file URL to load a local HTML file.

    b. Use loadHTMLString(...) to render simple string text.

c. Although not demonstrated here, you can also use
    loadData(...) to render NSData that you normally get
    from remote contents using NSURLConnection, which
    I will demonstrate later in the "NSURLConnection"
    section.

Listing 4-18. UIWebView Code for Loading a URL or String Text

```
class ViewController: ... {
  ...
  override func viewDidLoad() {
    ...
//    self.showWebPage(url: "http://pdachoice.com/me/webview")
    self.showWebPage(htmlString: "<H1>Hello UIWebView</H1>")
  }
  ...
  @IBOutlet weak var mWebView: UIWebView!
  func showWebPage(#url: String) {
    var req = NSURLRequest(URL: NSURL(string: url)!)
    self.mWebView.loadRequest(req)
  }

  func showWebPage(#htmlString: String) {
    self.mWebView.loadHTMLString(htmlString, baseURL: nil)
  }
  ...
```

4. To intercept UIWebView life-cycle events, implement the
    UIWebViewDelegate protocol, as shown in Listing 4-19.

Listing 4-19. UIWebViewDelegate Protocol

```
class ViewController: ... , UIWebViewDelegate {
  ...
  func webView(webView: UIWebView, shouldStartLoadWithRequest request:
  NSURLRequest, navigationType: UIWebViewNavigationType) -> Bool {
    // do the needful, like re-direct or intercept etc.
    return true; // false to stop http request
  }
  func webViewDidStartLoad(webView: UIWebView) {
    // do the needful, i.e., start UIActivityViewIndicator
    self.mActivityIndicator.startAnimating()
  }
  func webViewDidFinishLoad(webView: UIWebView) {
    // do the needful, i.e., stop  UIActivityViewIndicator
    self.mActivityIndicator.stopAnimating()
  }
  func webView(webView: UIWebView, didFailLoadWithError error: NSError) {
```

```
    // do something, i.e., show error alert
    self.mActivityIndicator.stopAnimating()
    var alert = UIAlertController(title: "Error", message: error.
    localizedDescription, preferredStyle: UIAlertControllerStyle.Alert)
    alert.addAction(UIAlertAction(title: "Close", style: UIAlertActionStyle.
    Cancel, handler: nil))
    self.presentViewController(alert, animated: true, completion: nil)
  }
  ...
```

Build and run the app to see iOS `UIWebView` in action. Now, even the iPad Air screen is too small (see Figure 4-37). You need a widget that scrolls content just like any browser does with HTML pages; you will implement this next.

Figure 4-37. UIWebView in the iPad Air emulator

ScrollView

Because of the smaller screen size on mobile devices, ScrollView is useful for displaying a content view larger than the physical display. To implement this in iOS, you use UIScrollView.

To make UIScrollView work with Auto Layout, it is easier to wrap all the widgets in a container view first, which will let you lay out the widgets in the container view as you normally would with Auto Layout.

The following steps demonstrate how you would normally do this with iOS's UIScrollView in the CommonWidgets app:

1. Using a single child view will simplify scrolling all the widgets in it. Select all widgets in the root view, select Embed In ➤ View from the Xcode menu bar to embed all these common widgets in a View (see Figure 4-38), and change this storyboard label to containerView.

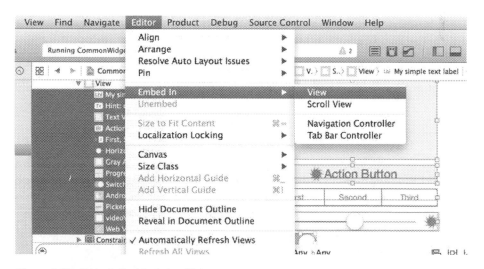

Figure 4-38. Embed all widgets in a View

2. Change View Controller Simulated Size to Fixed. The storyboard scene becomes shorter, with some widgets left out of the screen, as shown in Figure 4-39.

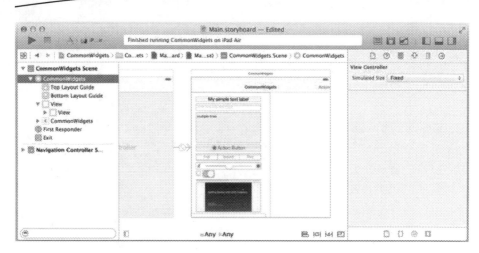

Figure 4-39. Change the scene to a fixed size

3.   With the `containerView` that contains all the widgets, you can scroll the `containerView` as a whole by embedding the `containerView` in UIScrollView. Select `containerView` first and embed it in a scroll view, as shown in Figure 4-40 (Editor ➤ Embed In ➤ Scroll View).

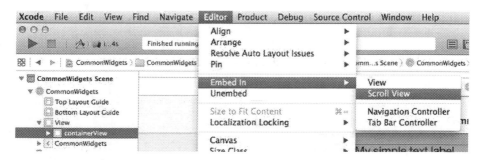

Figure 4-40. Embed containerView in a scroll view

4.   Open the Add New Constraints pop-up and pin the UIScrollView edges to the edge of the super view with zero spacing; then update the frame (see Figure 4-41).

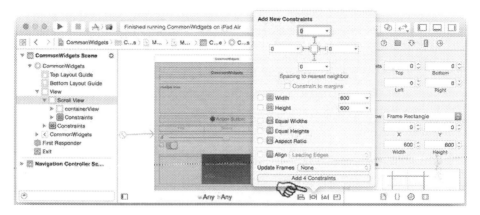

Figure 4-41. Set the UIScrollView constraint

5. The preceding operation shifts the `containerView`.
    In the `containerView` Size Inspector, reposition the
    `containerView` to (0,0) with a size of 600 (do not
    change the height).

6. `ScrollView` needs to know the content size, either
    explicitly or calculated from Auto Layout if you set up
    your constraints the right way. To make it adaptive to
    a size class, the next step is to add constraints from
    the content view to the scroll view:

    a. The Auto Layout constraints are repurposed for calculating
        the scrolling content size. You have to create Auto Layout
        constraints to pin the edges to the parent `UIScrollView`
        with zero spacing (see Figure 4-42).

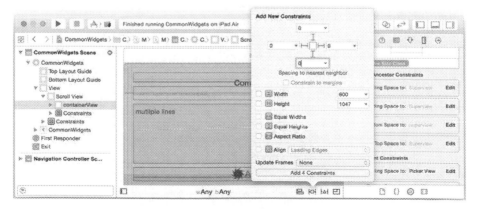

Figure 4-42. contentView pinned to UIScrollView with zero spacing

7. The content view width is not adaptive yet because the leading and trailing Auto Layout constraints to the scroll view created in the preceding step were repurposed for the scroll view contentSize. You can create the same constraints to views outside of the scroll view, that is, the root view.

    a. Connect the containerView view element in storyboard scene to your Swift code: the @IBOutlet mContainerView property.

    b. Currently, you cannot use a storyboard to add constraints to a parent's parent. You have to write code, as shown in Listing 4-20.

Listing 4-20. Pin contentView Edges to Screen/Root view Edges

```
class ViewController: ... {
  ...
  @IBOutlet var mContainerView: UIView!
  override func viewDidLoad() {
  ...
    var leftConstraint = NSLayoutConstraint(
      item: self.mContainerView,
      attribute: NSLayoutAttribute.Leading,
      relatedBy: NSLayoutRelation(rawValue: 0)!,
      toItem: self.view,
      attribute: NSLayoutAttribute.Leading,
      multiplier: 1.0,
      constant: 0)
    self.view.addConstraint(leftConstraint)

    var rightConstraint = NSLayoutConstraint(
      item: self.mContainerView,
      attribute: NSLayoutAttribute.Trailing,
      relatedBy: NSLayoutRelation(rawValue: 0)!,
      toItem: self.view,
      attribute: NSLayoutAttribute.Trailing,
      multiplier: 1.0,
      constant: 0)
    self.view.addConstraint(rightConstraint)
  ...
```

8. You can also set the widgets inside the containerView for Auto Layout so they adapt to different size classes.

Build and run the app to see iOS UIScrollView in action. You should be able to see all the widgets by scrolling the view up and down (see Figure 4-43).

 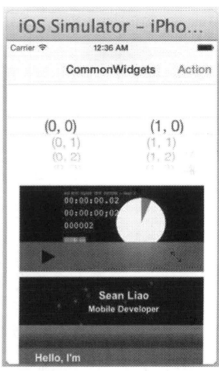

Figure 4-43. CommonWidgets with scrollable view

Animations

Back in the "old days," I cared a lot less about animation effects, but I think the evolution of iOS has definitely raised the bar. In iOS, you can animate UIView properties using the simple UIView animation API.

To learn by example, modify the existing UISegmentedControl. doScValueChanged(...) method, as shown in Listing 4-21, to create some animation effects using the UIView.animateWithDuration(...) method.

Listing 4-21. UIView.animateWithDuration(...)

```
...
@IBAction func doScValueChanged(sender: AnyObject) {
  var idx = self.mSegmentedController.selectedSegmentIndex
  self.logText("segment \(idx)")
  let center = self.mButton.center
  UIView.animateWithDuration(1, animations: { action in
    self.mButton.center = CGPoint(x: center.x, y: center.y / CGFloat(idx + 1))
    self.mButton.alpha = 1 / CGFloat(idx + 1)
    }, completion: { action in
```

```
UIView.animateWithDuration(1, delay: 0, usingSpringWithDamping: 0.5,
initialSpringVelocity: 0.5, options: .CurveEaseInOut,
  animations: { action in
    self.mButton.center = center
  }, completion: {  action in
    // do nothing
  })
})
}
...
```

The `UIView.animateWithDuration(...)` method has several overloaded variants that all work the same way. You can animate the following `UIView` properties by modifying them inside the animation block:

- `frame` for the viewing area
- `center` for position
- `transform` for scale and rotation
- `alpha` for transparency
- `backgroundColor`

Note, you cannot animate the `hidden` property directly. You would need to animate the `alpha` value to animate the fade-out or fade-in effects.

Save Data

WEB ANALOGY

Traditionally, a web app's front end is more of a thin client approach that saves data on the server side. You may find the topic more familiar to back-end implementations. Even in the front-end JavaScript development, the HTML5 local storage is good to store a small amount of user preferences as well.

Saving data is an essential programming task in almost all common programming platforms. In addition to transactional data, most of the mobile apps also save application states and user preferences so that users can resume their tasks later. Most of the native including desktop, iOS, and other mobile platforms provide several persistent storage options. The iOS SDK offers the following choices:

- User Defaults System

- File storage

- Core Data framework and SQLite database (not covered in this book)

Before diving into the first two options, you will create an Xcode project so that you can write code and visualize how these options work.

1. Launch Xcode, use the Single View Application template, and name the project **SaveData**.

2. Create a Navigation Bar with an `UIBarButtonItem` (see Figure 4-44):

   a. Select the View Controller in storyboard, and from the Xcode menu bar, select Editor ➤ Embed In ➤ Navigation Controller.

   b. In the Navigation Item Attributes Inspector, enter a Title of **SaveData**.

   c. Drag a `BarButtonItem` from the Object Library and drop it onto the Navigation Item in the View Controller scene. Update the Bar Item Title in the Attributes Inspector to **Delete**.

   d. Select the Bar Button Item and open the Assistant Editor to connect the selector outlet to your code. Name the `IBAction` **doDelete**.

3. Create a `UITextField` to get user input, as shown in Figure 4-44.

   a. Drag a `UITextField` onto the View Controller scene. In the Attributes Inspector, enter the placeholder **"Please save my inputs !!!"**.

   b. Add Auto Layout constraints to center the `UITextField` in the `View`.

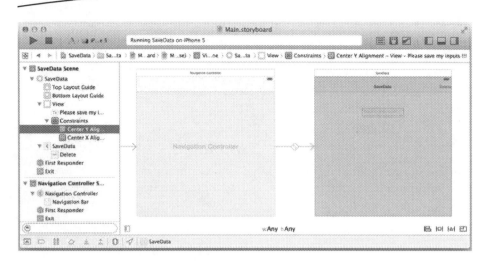

Figure 4-44. SaveData project storyboard

4. Open the Assistant Editor; in the UITextField
    Connections Inspector, connect the following outlets
    to your code:

    a. Connect Referencing Outlet to the IBOutlet property,
        mTextField.

    b. Connect delegate to your ViewController class.

5. Implement the UITextFieldDelegate protocol in the
    ViewController class and create the stubs that will
    trigger the retrieve, save, and delete code, as shown
    in Listing 4-22.

    a. Load the saved data in ViewController.viewDidLoad().

    b. Save the user input when the Return key is pressed.

    c. Give users a choice to delete any persistent data they
        created.

Listing 4-22. SaveData ViewController

```
class ViewController: UIViewController, UITextFieldDelegate {
  ...
  let STORAGE_KEY = "key"
  @IBOutlet weak var mTextField: UITextField!
  override func viewDidLoad() {
    ...
```

```
  self.mTextField.text = self.retrieveUserInput()
}

@IBAction func doDelete(sender: AnyObject) {
  self.deleteUserInput();
}

func textFieldShouldReturn(textField: UITextField!) -> Bool {
  ...
  self.saveUserInput(self.mTextField.text)
  return true
}

func saveUserInput(str: String) {
  // TODO
}

func retrieveUserInput() -> String? {
  // TODO
  return nil
}

func deleteUserInput() {
  // TODO
}
...
```

Nothing is new yet. Build and run the SaveData project (see Figure 4-45).

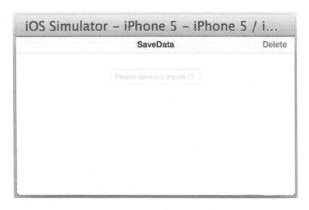

Figure 4-45. *The SaveData project display*

Without completing the method stubs, this new project exhibits a common problem that can be observed in the following three steps:

1. Enter something in the input text field.

2. Exit the app.

3. Relaunch the app. The previous input is gone!

For typical app settings or user preferences, users are not happy if they need to reenter them every time they launch the app. The app needs to save the data and load it when the app restarts.

NSUserDefaults

You typically store a small amount of nonsensitive user preferences or application settings so that your users don't need to reenter the setting all the time in web apps. You can store this data in a server database, in HTML5 browser local storage, or in cookies. In iOS, you use the NSUserDefaults class to interface with iOS's User Defaults System for the same purpose. NSUserDefaults takes care of data caching and syncing for developers. It is easy to use, and its performance is already optimized.

The values to be managed in the iOS User Defaults System can be primitives or the so-called property list object (for example, NSData, NSString, NSNumber, NSDate, NSArray, or NSDictionary). For NSArray and NSDictionary objects, their contents must be property list objects as well.

Continue with the SaveData project. You will fix the problem you just observed.

1. Create the convenient methods that save, retrieve, and delete data using the NSUserDefaults API (see Listing 4-23):

    a. Get the NSUserDefaults object.

    b. You want to accumulate multiple updates and call synchronize() to send the batched updates to the User Defaults System storage.

Listing 4-23. Save, Retrieve, and Delete in User Defaults System

```
class ViewController: UIViewController, UITextFieldDelegate {
  ...
  let userDefaults = NSUserDefaults.standardUserDefaults()
  func saveUserdefault(data: AnyObject, forKey: String) {
    userDefaults.setObject(data, forKey: forKey)
    userDefaults.synchronize()
  }
```

```
func retrieveUserdefault(key: String) -> String? {
  var obj = userDefaults.stringForKey(key)
  return obj
}

func deleteUserDefault(key: String) {
  self.userDefaults.removeObjectForKey(key)
}
...
```

2.   Earlier, you already created the stubs that are wired
     to the right events. Call the convenient methods
     just created to complete the persistent code
     (see Listing 4-24).

Listing 4-24. Save, Retrieve, and Delete Using the User Defaults System

```
class ViewController: UIViewController, UITextFieldDelegate {
  ...
  func saveUserInput(str: String) {
    self.saveUserdefault(str, forKey: STORAGE_KEY)
  }

  func retrieveUserInput() -> String? {
    return self.retrieveUserdefault(STORAGE_KEY)
  }

  func deleteUserInput() {
    self.deleteUserDefault(STORAGE_KEY)
  }
  ...
```

Relaunch the SaveData project and repeat the failed test case. You should
no longer need to reenter the name when reopening the app.

File Storage

WEB ANALOGY

This is commonly available for back-end server development but not available for front-end
web development.

The iOS SDK provides system APIs to interface with the file system. In iOS, you commonly use the following API:

- You can use the `NSFileManager` class.

- The `NSString`, `NSArray`, `NSDictionary`, and `NSData` Foundation classes also have convenient methods to store and retrieve themselves from file systems.

NSFileManager

If you need to perform any file-related tasks to manipulate `File` and `Directory`, `NSFileManager` provides the API to do the work. You need to specify the file path or file URL for the destination file and specify the `NSData` object for the file contents.

To show and to learn by example, use `NSFileManager` to achieve the same save/retrieve/delete purpose.

1. Create the convenient methods that save, retrieve, and delete data using the `NSFileManager` API (see Listing 4-25).

    a. Get the `NSFileManager` object.

    b. Use `NSHomeDirectory().stringByAppendingPathComponent(...)` to build the iOS file path.

> **Note** Each app can write only to certain a certain folder inside the application home (for example, the `Documents` folder). The most common error is probably trying to create a file in the wrong place.

    c. `NSFileManager` deals with `NSData`, which can be converted to common Foundation data types (for example, String, array, and dictionary).

Listing 4-25. Manage Data in Files Using NSFileManager

```
class ViewController: UIViewController, UITextFieldDelegate {
  ...
  let fileMgr = NSFileManager.defaultManager()
  func saveToFile(str: String, file: String) {
    var path = NSHomeDirectory().stringByAppendingPathComponent
("Documents").stringByAppendingPathComponent(file)
```

```
  var data = str.dataUsingEncoding(NSUTF8StringEncoding)
  var ok = fileMgr.createFileAtPath(path, contents: data, attributes: nil)
}

func retrieveFromFile(file: String) -> String? {
  var path = NSHomeDirectory().stringByAppendingPathComponent
  ("Documents").stringByAppendingPathComponent(file)
  if let data = fileMgr.contentsAtPath(path) {
    return NSString(data:data, encoding: NSUTF8StringEncoding)
  }

  return nil
}

func deleteFile(file: String) {
  var path = NSHomeDirectory().stringByAppendingPathComponent
  ("Documents").stringByAppendingPathComponent(file)
  var ok = fileMgr.removeItemAtPath(path, error: nil)
}
...
```

2. Call the convenient methods just created to complete the persistent code that uses NSFileManager (see Listing 4-26).

Listing 4-26. Save, Retrieve, and Delete Using NSFileManager

```
class ViewController: UIViewController, UITextFieldDelegate {
  ...
  func saveUserInput(str: String) {
//    self.saveUserdefault(str, forKey: STORAGE_KEY)
    self.saveToFile(str, file: STORAGE_KEY)
  }

  func retrieveUserInput() -> String? {
//    return self.retrieveUserdefault(STORAGE_KEY)
    return self.retrieveFromFile(STORAGE_KEY)
  }

  func deleteUserInput() {
//    self.deleteUserDefault(STORAGE_KEY)
    self.deleteFile(STORAGE_KEY)
  }
  ...
```

Generally, you only need to use NSFileManager directly for pure file-system operations such as inspecting file attributes or iterating through files in directories because iOS Foundation data types contain convenient methods to interface with File for saving and retrieving themselves. Listing 4-27 depicts simpler code that saves and retrieves the string itself.

Listing 4-27. Save String Using Foundation Class API

```
func saveToFile(str: String, file: String) {
  var path = ...
  var error: NSError?
  str.writeToFile(path, atomically: true, encoding: NSUTF8StringEncoding,
  error: &error)
}

func retrieveFromFile(file: String) -> String? {
  var path = ...
  var error: NSError?
  var str = String(contentsOfFile: path, encoding: NSUTF8StringEncoding,
  error: &error)

  return str
}
```

You can find the same writeToFile(...) and init(...) methods in
NSDictionary, NSArray, and NSData for saving and retrieving themselves. Just
as a quick exercise, Listing 4-28 serves the same purpose as Listing 4-27.

Listing 4-28. Save NSDictionary Using Foundation Class API

```
let KEY_JSON = "aKey"
func saveJsonToFile(str: String, file: String) {
  var path = NSHomeDirectory().stringByAppendingPathComponent
  ("Documents").stringByAppendingPathComponent(file)
  // one enry dict, for sure can be more
  var json = NSDictionary(objects: [str], forKeys: [KEY_JSON])
  json.writeToFile(path, atomically: true)
}

func retrieveJsonFromFile(file: String) -> String? {
  var path = NSHomeDirectory().stringByAppendingPathComponent
  ("Documents").stringByAppendingPathComponent(file)
  var ser = NSDictionary(contentsOfFile: path)!
  return ser[KEY_JSON] as String?
}
```

This is particularly useful when dealing with JSON messages because most
remote messages are in JSON format nowadays.

Networking and Using Remote Service

A typical client-server solution hosts information on the server side, while
client apps either fetch data from the server and present it to users in
meaningful ways or collect data from the users to submit to the server. You

probably have heard the buzzwords *mobile commerce* or *m-commerce* a lot recently. To describe them in simple terms, mobile apps fetch product items from a server and then submit the purchase orders to the server via the Internet. From a mobile-apps programming perspective, this is really not new at all. It is still a client-server programming topic using HTTP GET/POST, which is what most e-commerce sites do.

I will talk about JSON messages and RESTful services for mobile apps specifically because of their popularity versus traditional SOAP-based web services.

Perform Network Operations in Background

For apps with a user interface, you want to perform I/O tasks or network-related code in the background and do UI updates in the UI main thread. Otherwise, the app appears to the user to lag because the UI thread is blocked, waiting for the task to finish. This principle applies to iOS, Android, and probably any UI platforms. Generally, when interfacing with a remote server, you want to fetch data in the background thread. When the remote data is received, your UI code presents the data on the screen in the UI thread.

To show how to achieve the objectives in iOS by example, you will create a simple iOS app, as shown in Figure 4-46, to demonstrate some basic RESTful client code that consumes remote RESTful services.

- When the GET or POST button is selected, the app sends an HTTP GET or POST to the server in a background thread.

- When the HTTP response is received, the app renders the data on the user interface.

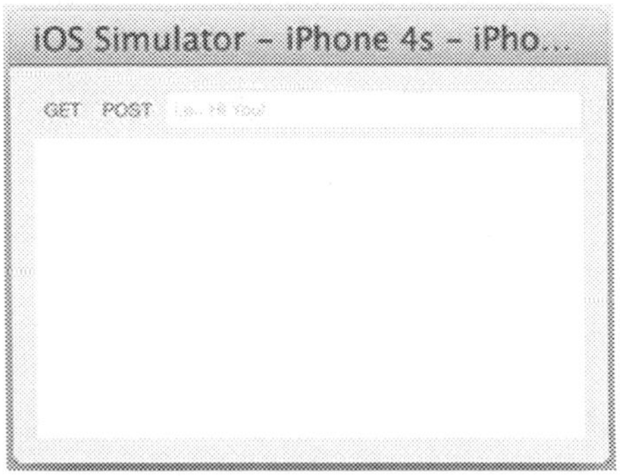

Figure 4-46. The iOS RestClient app

Create a new Xcode project.

1. Launch Xcode, use the Single View Application template, and name the project **RestClient**.

2. Draw your storyboard with the following widgets (see Figure 4-47):

    a. A UIButton to invoke an HTTP GET

    b. A UIButton to invoke an HTTP POST

    c. A UITextField to take user input

    d. A UIWebView to render the HTTP response

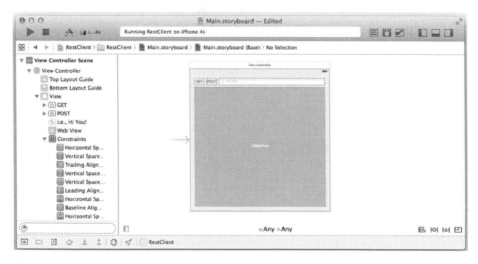

Figure 4-47. RestClient storyboard

3. Connect the following storyboard outlets to your code (see Listing 4-29):

    a. Connect the GET button Touch Down event to your doGet()IBAction method.

    b. Connect the POST button Touch Down event to your doPost()IBAction method.

    c. Connect the UITextField delegate outlet to the ViewController class.

    d. Connect the UIWebView delegate to the ViewController class.

e. Connect the text field New Referencing Outlet to the
    ViewController mTextField IBOutlet property.

f. Connect the webview New Referencing Outlet to the
    ViewController mWebView IBOutlet property.

Listing 4-29. RestClient Preparation Code

```
class ViewController: UIViewController, UITextFieldDelegate,
UIWebViewDelegate {

  @IBOutlet weak var mWebView: UIWebView!
  @IBOutlet weak var mTextField: UITextField!

  override func viewDidLoad() {
    super.viewDidLoad()
    // Do any additional setup after loading the view ...
  }

  func textFieldShouldReturn(textField: UITextField!) -> Bool {
    textField.resignFirstResponder();
    return true
  }

  @IBAction func doGet(sender: AnyObject) {
  }

  @IBAction func doPost(sender: AnyObject) {
  }
}
```

Nothing is new yet; you just used the same storyboard tasks and the same
process of connecting the outlets to your code with the method stubs. You
will fill the main topics in these stubs next.

RESTful Service Using HTTP

Most of the RESTful services support the HTTP and HTTPS protocols. To
retrieve data from a RESTful services, use HTTP GET to fetch a remote HTML
file. You can use an HTTP GET to fetch an HTML document from mobile
apps, too—or it can fetch any data, such as raw bytes, an XML or JSON
document, and so forth.

To submit user input, you often use an HTML form to submit form data
from an HTML page to HTTP servers. The form data is transmitted using
the HTTP POST method. This is common in iOS apps as well. Technically
speaking, you can also send a query string to an HTTP server using the

HTTP GET method, just as some web pages do. In this case, you can simply build the URL with query strings and use the HTTP GET method to send data to your server. It is a design decision that you will make by understanding the usages and conventions of GET versus POST. The key is to design the interface so both your mobile clients and the server can understand it.

NSURLConnection

To interface with the HTTP protocol in iOS, you can use the NSURLConnection class to send GET and POST URL requests. The API is fairly similar to JAVA's HttpUrlConnection.

Continue with the RestClient project and add code to send HTTP requests by doing the following:

1. Implement the IBAction doGet() method to send the HTTP GET request and to get data from the HTTP response (see Listing 4-30).

    a. Create an NSMutableURLRequest object.

> **Note** You commonly escape/encode the URL path or query string.

    b. Set the HTTP method to GET.

> **Note** An HTTP method is case-sensitive according to the HTTP protocol specs.

    c. Set the accept header, which is commonly used for content negotiation (for example, text/html, json/application, and so on).

> **Note** The sample echo service supports "text/html", "text/plain", and "application/json" content types. To demonstrate the content negotiation visually, I chose to use a UIWebView widget to render the server response and specify "text/html". In general, "application/json" is more suitable for data exchange.

    d. NSURLConnection.sendAsynchronousRequest sends an asynchronous HTTP request and receives the HTTP response in the completionHandler closure in the UI main thread.

Listing 4-30. HTTP GET

```
let URL_TEST = "http://pdachoice.com/ras/service/echo/"
@IBAction func doGet(sender: AnyObject) {
  UIApplication.sharedApplication().networkActivityIndicatorVisible = true
  var text = self.mTextField.text.
  stringByAddingPercentEncodingWithAllowedCharacters(NSCharacterSet.
  URLHostAllowedCharacterSet())

  var url = URL_TEST + text!
  var urlRequest = NSMutableURLRequest(URL: NSURL(string: url)!)
  urlRequest.HTTPMethod = "GET"
  urlRequest.setValue("text/html", forHTTPHeaderField: "accept")

  NSURLConnection.sendAsynchronousRequest(urlRequest, queue:
  NSOperationQueue.mainQueue(),
    completionHandler: {(resp: NSURLResponse!, data: NSData!, error:
    NSError!) -> Void in
      UIApplication.sharedApplication().networkActivityIndicatorVisible = false
      println(resp.textEncodingName)
      self.mWebView.loadData(data, MIMEType: resp.MIMEType,
      textEncodingName: resp.textEncodingName, baseURL: nil)
  })
}
```

    1. Implement the IBAction doPost() method to send an HTTP POST to post data to the server and receive an HTTP response (see Listing 4-31). Almost the same as sending HTTP GET, you use NSURLConnection.sendAsynchronousRequest to send asynchronous HTTP messages, except you set the HTTP method to POST.

        a. Make sure to set the HTTP method to POST.

        b. POST data has the same format as a query string, but you want to encode it to put in the HTTP Body, the same way you do in Android.

        c. To parse JSON content or create a JSON object, NSJSONSerialization is your friend. You want to convert the JSON object to NSDictionary or the JSON array to NSArray.

Listing 4-31. HTTP POST

```
@IBAction func doPost(sender: AnyObject) {
  UIApplication.sharedApplication().networkActivityIndicatorVisible = true
  var text = self.mTextField.text.
  stringByAddingPercentEncodingWithAllowedCharacters(
    NSCharacterSet.URLQueryAllowedCharacterSet())
  var queryString = "echo=" + text!;
  var formData = queryString.dataUsingEncoding(NSUTF8StringEncoding)!
  var urlRequest = NSMutableURLRequest(URL: NSURL(string: URL_TEST)!)
  urlRequest.HTTPMethod = "POST"
  urlRequest.HTTPBody = formData

  urlRequest.setValue("application/json", forHTTPHeaderField: "accept")

  NSURLConnection.sendAsynchronousRequest(urlRequest,
    queue: NSOperationQueue.mainQueue(),
    completionHandler: {(resp: NSURLResponse!, data: NSData!, error:
    NSError!) -> Void in
      UIApplication.sharedApplication().networkActivityIndicatorVisible = false

      println(NSString(data: data, encoding: NSUTF8StringEncoding))

      var json = NSJSONSerialization.JSONObjectWithData(data, options:
        NSJSONReadingOptions.AllowFragments, error: nil) as NSDictionary
      var echo = json["echo"] as String
      self.mWebView.loadHTMLString(echo, baseURL: nil)
  })
}
```

> **Note** SERVER_URL = "http://pdachoice.com/ras/service/echo"
> is a simple web service that echoes back the path parameter. Desktop browsers
> are fully capable of rendering plain text as well as HTML documents. You can
> use a desktop browser to verify the data from the server.

Build and run the RestClient project and enter **Hi you!** to see the app in
action. The simple echo service with the GET method actually responded
in HTML format, <html><body><h1>Hi you!</h1></body></html>, which is
rendered as shown in Figure 4-48.

Figure 4-48. *RestClient doGet and doPost responses*

Summary

This chapter introduced the most common programming component mappings from Android to iOS.

- User interface and UI widgets
- Persistent storage options
- Network and remote services with JSON

Many meaningful apps only ever deal with the simple components discussed in this chapter. You will see how to apply these guidelines to build a simple but complete utility app from start to finish in the next chapter.

Part 3

Finishing Touches

Chapter 5

Pulling It All Together

Thus far in this book, you have learned about many discrete mobile topics and created more than ten Xcode projects. Those topics were purposely implemented in individual Xcode projects with few classes. In Chapter 3, you learned the top-down development approach of using the storyboard to break the whole app into model-view-controller (MVC) content view and view controller pairs. In Chapter 4, you learned how to port smaller individual components, including user interface (UI), create read update delete (CRUD), and remote operations, piece by piece. However, all those topics were designed to be self-contained without dependencies so they could serve as independent instructions.

In the real programming world, it is the combination of features and use cases that makes your app useful and entertaining. You will surely need to understand more than one topic to complete a meaningful app. In this chapter, you will implement a simple but meaningful Swift app from start to finish using the mapping topics from Chapters 3 and 4. Nothing will be new; you will repeat the same top-down development approach as you have been using and implement one piece at a time.

Perhaps there is one thing new that I have not yet mentioned explicitly: which piece should be developed first and then what comes next. For any app, including web apps, you should go through the same thought process: you should decide the dependencies of the pieces and try to reduce the dependencies along the way. After all, there is really no right or wrong way to do it.

Again, to learn by example, your goal is to implement a RentalROI iOS app. Figure 5-1 shows the completed iOS app you will be creating.

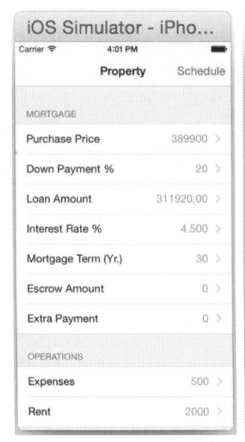

Figure 5-1. *RentalROI screens*

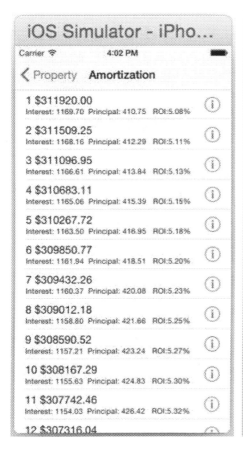

Figure 5-1. (continued)

This RentalROI app performs the following tasks:

- Every time a user enters new rental property parameters, user input is saved using SharedPreferences.

- The amortization schedule is calculated on the remote server. The iOS client simply calls the remote service to get the amortization schedules and stores the data locally.

- If a saved amortization schedule exists, the app uses it instead of making a remote service call.

> **Note**   This is just for exercise purposes. It would be better to calculate the amortization schedules locally without using the remote service—then you wouldn't need to persist the result.

First, you'll create a new Xcode project using the Single View Application template; name it **RentalROI**. You will be following the same porting approaches you used in Chapters 3 and 4.

Structure Your App

As usual, use top-down approach starting with storyboard tasks. Your first step is to create the Xcode storyboard as instructed in Chapter 3.

- Draw the storyboard scenes for each content view and connect UI widgets to the custom `UIViewController` that pairs with the storyboard scenes.

- Choose a navigation pattern and connect the storyboard scenes together with segues.

This will result in a runnable iOS app with all the content views and the view controller classes' skeletons connected using the appropriate screen navigation pattern.

Draw Storyboard Scenes

You can clearly see four content views in Figure 5-1, and you will need to draw four storyboard scenes in `Main.storyboard`, covered next.

Edit Text Screen

In no particular order, let's start with the simplest one, the second screen in Figure 5-1. You want to add a `UITextField` to the storyboard scene (see Chapter 4 for the detailed instructions).

1. Drag a `UITextField` from the Object Library to the view and update its attributes in the Attributes Inspector, as shown in Figure 5-2.

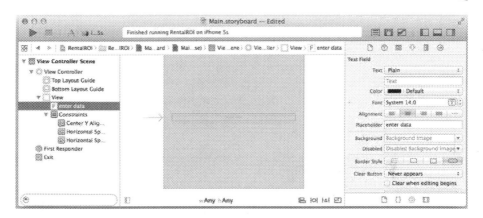

Figure 5-2. EditTextView storyboard scene

2. Center it vertically and add some space to the
    leading and trailing spaces (for example, enter **20**).

3. Create a bare-bones Swift EditTextViewController
    class that extends from UIViewController
    (see Listing 5-1).

4. To pair with the storyboard scene, enter the custom
    class name in the Identity Inspector.

5. In the Connections Inspector, connect the delegate
    outlet and New Referencing Outlet to your code
    (see Chapter 4 for step-by-step operations).

Listing 5-1. EditTextViewController

```
import UIKit

class EditTextViewController : UIViewController, UITextFieldDelegate {
  @IBOutlet weak var mEditText: UITextField!
}
```

Rental Property Info Screen

Continue drawing the next content view in no particular order (for example,
draw the Property screen, shown in Figure 5-1). To achieve the list view
L&F, you should use UITableViewController (see Chapter 3 for the detailed
instructions).

1. Drag a Table View Controller from the Object
    Library and drop it onto the storyboard editor to
    create a storyboard scene.

2. Select the Table View object and set the Style
    attribute to Grouped in the Attributes Inspector
    (see Figure 5-3).

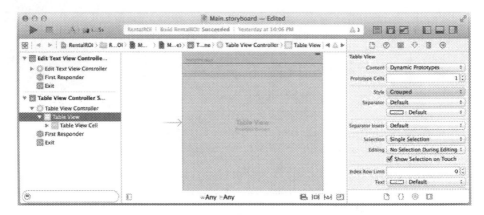

Figure 5-3. Creating a Table View scene

3. Select the Table View Cell object and update the
    attributes in the Attributes Inspector (see Figure 5-4).

Figure 5-4. Right Detail, Table View Cell

    a. *Style*: Select Right Detail.

    b. *Identifier*: Enter **aCell**.

    c. Create a bare-bones Swift
        RentalPropertyViewController class that extends
        from UITableViewController (see Listing 5-2). To
        pair with the storyboard scene, enter the custom
        class name in the Identity Inspector.

Listing 5-2. RentalPropertyViewController

```
import UIKit
class RentalPropertyViewController : UITableViewController {

}
```

Amortization Screen

Continue drawing the next content view in no particular order (for example, the Amortization screen, shown in Figure 5-1). It shows a list of amortization items, and a natural choice for this is UITableViewController.

1. Drag a Table View Controller from the Object Library and drop it onto the storyboard editor to create a storyboard scene.

2. Select the Table View Cell. In the Attributes Inspector, update the following attributes:

   a. *Style*: Select Subtitle.

   b. *Identifier*: Enter **aCell**.

3. Create a bare-bones Swift AmortizationViewController class that extends from UITableViewController (see Listing 5-3). To pair with the storyboard scene, enter the custom class name in the Identity Inspector.

Listing 5-3. AmortizationViewController

```
import UIKit
class AmortizationViewController: UITableViewController {

}
```

Monthly Details Screen

Move on to drawing the last content view, Monthly Details (shown in Figure 5-1). It has a listlike look and feel but does not really show list items. You can choose to implement this screen with labels for each line items in iOS, or you can choose to use a UITableView, as in RentalPropertyViewController. There is actually a better choice, though: using UITableViewController with static cells, with one static cell for each line.

1. Drag a Table View Controller from the Object Library and drop it onto the storyboard editor to create a storyboard scene.

2. Select the Table View to update the attributes in the Attributes Inspector, as shown in Figure 5-5.

    a. *Content*: Select Static Cells.

    b. *Sections*: Enter **2**.

    c. *Style*: Select Grouped.

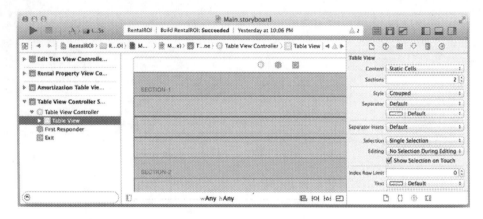

Figure 5-5. Static Cells Table View

3. The Monthly Details screen contains Mortgage Payment and Investment sections. You need to update the section title and add Table View Cell objects to both sections, as shown in Figure 5-6.

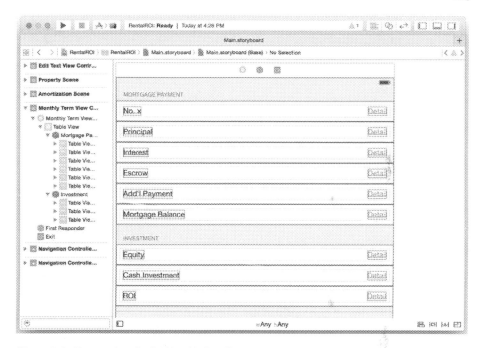

Figure 5-6. Two sections in the Monthly Details screen

4. To update the section title, select the Table View section and update the Header attributes in the Attributes Inspector:

    a. *Section 1*: Enter **Mortgage Payment**.

    b. *Section 2*: Enter **Investment**.

5. Since all the Table View Cells in this view are designed to have the same style, it is easier just to create one and duplicate it. You may keep the first Table View Cell and delete the rest.

    a. Select the Table View Cell and update the Style value to Right Detail.

    b. Select the Mortgage Payment section and update the number of rows to 6.

    c. You need three Table View Cells for Section 2. You may repeat the preceding steps or copy and paste in the storyboard editor.

    d. Update all the Table View Cell titles, as shown in Figure 5-6.

6. Create a bare-bones Swift
   MonthlyTermViewController class that extends from
   UITableViewController. To pair with the storyboard
   scene, enter the custom class name in the Identity
   Inspector.

7. Open the Assistant Editor and connect the first Table
   View Cell left text label and each Table View Cell right
   detail label, respectively, to your code's IBOutlet
   properties, as shown in Listing 5-4.

Listing 5-4. MonthlyTermViewController IBOutlet Properties

```swift
import UIKit
class MonthlyTermViewController : UITableViewController {

  @IBOutlet weak var mPaymentNo: UILabel!
  @IBOutlet weak var mTotalPmt: UILabel!
  @IBOutlet weak var mPrincipal: UILabel!
  @IBOutlet weak var mInterest: UILabel!
  @IBOutlet weak var mEscrow: UILabel!
  @IBOutlet weak var mAddlPmt: UILabel!
  @IBOutlet weak var mBalance: UILabel!
  @IBOutlet weak var mEquity: UILabel!
  @IBOutlet weak var mCashInvested: UILabel!
  @IBOutlet weak var mRoi: UILabel!
}
```

Figure 5-7 depicts the results of the storyboard scenes' tasks.

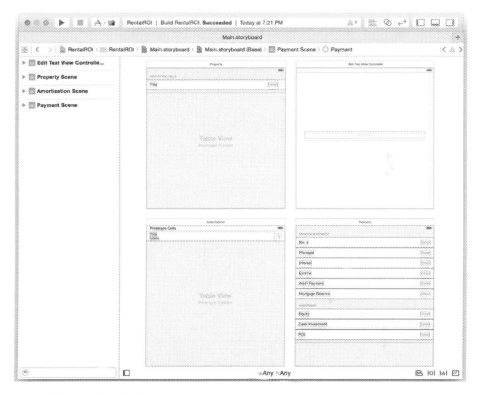

Figure 5-7. *Four RentalROI scenes*

Choose a Screen Navigation Pattern

When choosing appropriate navigation patterns, you will get good ideas from using wireframes. You normally need more than one pattern, such as a navigation stack plus navigation tabs. In this RentalROI app, you want to be able go back to a previous scene from Monthly Details to Amortization List to Property. The popular navigation stack navigation pattern is perfect for this intended behavior (see Chapter 3 for more information). For going to and from the Edit Text scene, you can choose a different navigation pattern that shows a stronger relationship to the originating context. Dialog or the iOS pop-over is the best choice (see Chapter 3).

Your immediate mission is to add the navigation patterns and draw storyboard segues to connect all the storyboard scenes to one another. Figure 5-8 shows the final storyboard with all the scenes connected.

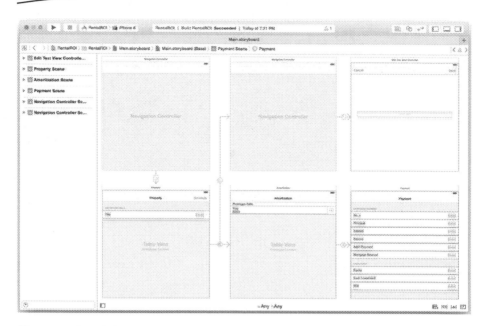

Figure 5-8. RentalROI-connected scenes

Continue with the storyboard tasks by doing the following (see Chapter 3 for more detailed instructions):

1. Select `RentalPropertyViewController` in the storyboard editor and embed it in a `UINavigationController` (see Figure 3-33 in Chapter 3 for step-by-step instructions).

    a. Make sure Is Initial View Controller is checked in the Navigation Controller's Attributes Inspector.

    b. Select the Navigation Item in `RentalPropertyViewController` to update the Title attribute to Property in the Attributes Inspector.

    c. Add a right BarButtonItem to the Property Navigation Item in `RentalPropertyViewController`. Also, update the button's Title attribute to Schedule in the BarButtonItem Attributes Inspector.

    d. Connect the Schedule BarButtonItem action outlet in the Connections Inspector to your code, such as `doSchedule(...)`.

2. Connect a Manual Segue from `RentalPropertyViewController` to `AmortizationViewController`.

   a. *Segue*: Show (for example, Push)

   b. *Identifier*: AmortizationTable

3. Connect a Manual Segue from `RentalPropertyViewController` to `EditTextViewController`.

   a. *Segue*: Present As Popover

   b. *Identifier*: EditText

   c. *Anchor*: Table View

   d. *Directions*: none (uncheck all)

4. Connect a Manual Segue from `AmortizationViewController` to `MonthlyTermViewController`.

   a. *Segue*: Show (for example, Push)

   b. *Identifier*: MonthlyTerm

5. Add Navigation Item to `AmortizationViewController` and `MonthlyTermViewController`, as shown in Figure 5-8.

   a. Drag a Navigation Item from the Object Library and drop it onto the controller in the storyboard document outline.

   b. Update the Navigation Item titles, respectively (for example, Amortization and Payment).

6. Since you are not showing the
    `EditTextViewController` with the navigation pattern,
    `EditTextViewController` doesn't have a Navigation
    Item for Title or BarButtonItem like the rest of the
    storyboard scenes. You can draw a `UINavigationBar`
    as usual by dragging one from the Object Library, or,
    more commonly, you can simply embed it in another
    `UINavigationController`.

    a. Select the view controller and select Editor ➤
        Embedded In ➤ Navigation Controller from the
        Xcode Editor menu.

    b. Add a right BarButtonItem. Set the Title attribute to
        Save and connect the action outlet to your code,
        such as `doSave(...)`.

    c. Add a left BarButtonItem. Update the Title attribute
        to be Cancel and connect the action outlet to your
        code, such as `doCancel(...)`.

You should have a storyboard with all scenes connected with segues, as
shown in Figure 5-8.

Business Object

In object oriented programming, you create classes to present the business
domain. You define properties to encapsulate the object attributes and methods
for behaviors in the classes. After finishing the storyboard tasks, you naturally
gain a better understanding of the business domain and the attributes you
need to deal with. You don't have to discover all of them at once. You simply
create the business object when you discover any. For this RentalROI app, you
only need a class that presents the rental property. Let's create a Swift class
skeleton for the `RentalProperty` business object class first (see Listing 5-5).

Listing 5-5. RentalProperty.swift Skeleton

```
import Foundation
public class RentalProperty {

}
```

For its attributes and behaviors, you might see some from the storyboard
immediately, but you normally would not know them all in the beginning.
You will discover them along the way and just fill in the blanks when you
discover any.

Application Resources

Like with any GUI apps, you need images or digital assets to dress up the app. You also want to externalize strings to avoid coding these display texts directly. Do the following to implement the application resources (see Chapter 4) in this Xcode project:

1. All the display text needs to be externalized, as shown in Listing 5-6.

    a. In Xcode, select the Supporting Files folder to create a new file (⌘+N) in it, and follow the on-screen instructions to select iOS ➤ Resource ➤ Strings File. Name the file **Localizable.strings**.

    b. Define key-value pairs. You will access the value by the key from your Swift code.

Listing 5-6. Externalized Text Translation

```
"app_name" = "RentalROI";
"label_schedule" = "Schedule";
"label_property" = "Property";
"label_Amortization" = "Amortization";
"label_monthlydetails" = "Monthly Details";
"button_next" = "Next";

/* RentalPropertyView */
"mortgage" = "MORTGAGE";
"operations" = "OPERATIONS";
"purchasePrice" = "Purchase Price";
"downPayment" = "Down Payment %";
"loanAmount" = "Loan Amount";
"interestRate" = "Interest Rate %";
"mortgageTerm" = "Mortgage Term (Yr.)";
"escrowAmount" = "Escrow Amount";
"extraPayment" = "Extra Payment";
"expenses" = "Expenses";
"rent" = "Rent";

/* EditTextView */
"save" = "Save";
"editTextSize" = "15";

/* Monthly Details */
"MortgagePayment" = "MORTGAGE PAYMENT";
"no" = "No.";
"Principal" = "Principal";
"interest" = "Interest";
```

```
"escrow" = "Escrow";
"addlPayment" = "Add\'l Payment";
"mortgageBalance" = "Mortgage Balance";
"equity" = "Equity";
"cashInvest" = "Cash Investment";
"roi" = "ROI";
```

2. You should use the Xcode assets catalog to manage images. In this app, you need only one image: the application icon, `ic_launcher.png`. You can do it in the same way for any other images.

    a. Create `ic120.png`, `ic180.png`, `ic76.png`, and `ic152.png`.

    b. Select `Images.xcassets` and `AppIcon` in the Xcode assets catalog and drag the four files you just made into the appropriate slots, as shown in Figure 5-9: `ic120.png` for iPhone 2x, `ic180.png` for iPhone 3x, `ic76.png` for iPad 1x, and `ic152.png` for iPad 2x.The image resolution must match exactly or Xcode will give you warnings.

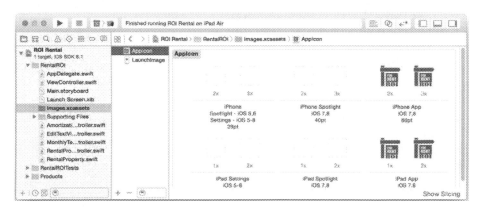

Figure 5-9. Xcode project AppIcon

Implement Piece by Piece

You have all the Swift class files, storyboards, and external assets in place. Your next step is to fill in the class by implementing methods. You will start to see how your code works piece by piece!

Normally, you would discover the methods by analyzing the intended behaviors per use cases. For the purposes of this book, I will go over the existing classes one at a time, focusing on iOS SDK topics instead.

RentalProperty

RentalProperty is the model class that encapsulates the business knowledge in terms of property and mortgage attributes, and so on. Since we going to persist these attributes, I chose to implement the persistent storage logic directly inside the model class. Let's start implementing the RentalProperty Swift class.

1. The Swift stored properties represent the application states (see Listing 5-7). All the attributes can be visualized in the Rental Property scene in the storyboard.

2. This app deals with one rental property at a time. The singleton pattern is commonly used in object-oriented code. This is how you do it in Swift:

   a. Declare a shared instance as a private static type property in the inner struct.

   b. Make the initializer private to prevent multiple instances from being created.

   c. Create a public class method to access the shared instance inside the inner strut.

Listing 5-7. The RentalProperty Class Singleton Implementation

```
import Foundation

public class RentalProperty {

    // 1. Swift stored properties to keep the application states
    var purchasePrice = 0.0;
    var loanAmt = 0.0;
    var interestRate = 5.0;
    var numOfTerms = 30;
    var escrow = 0.0;
    var extra = 0.0;
    var expenses = 0.0;
    var rent = 0.0;

    struct MyStatic {
        static let KEY_AMO_SAVED = "KEY_AMO_SAVED";
        static let KEY_PROPERTY = "KEY_PROPERTY";
        // 2a. singleton impl
        private static var _sharedInstance = RentalProperty()
    }
```

```
  // 2b. singleton impl, private initializer
  private init() {

  }

  // 2c. singleton accessor
  class func sharedInstance() -> RentalProperty {
    return MyStatic._sharedInstance
  }
  ...
}
```

3. Use NSUserDefaults to create the following utility methods in the RentalProperty.swift methods, as shown in Listing 5-8 (see Chapter 4).

Listing 5-8. Create Save Data Utility Methods

```
class RentalProperty {
  ...
  let userDefaults = NSUserDefaults.standardUserDefaults()
  private func saveUserdefault(data:AnyObject, forKey:String) -> Bool{
    userDefaults.setObject(data, forKey: forKey)
    return userDefaults.synchronize()
  }

  private func retrieveUserdefault(key: String) -> AnyObject? {
    var obj: AnyObject? = userDefaults.objectForKey(key)
    return obj
  }

  private func deleteUserDefault(key: String) {
    self.userDefaults.removeObjectForKey(key)
  }
  ...
```

4. Implement the load() method that loads the saved RentalProperty object from storage, as shown in Listing 5-9.

Listing 5-9. Loading RentalProperty Object from Storage

```
class RentalProperty {
  ...
  func load() -> Bool {
    var data = retrieveUserdefault(MyStatic.KEY_PROPERTY) as NSDictionary?
    if var jo = data {
      self.purchasePrice = jo["purchasePrice"] as Double
      self.loanAmt = jo["loanAmt"] as Double
      self.interestRate = jo["interestRate"] as Double
```

```
    self.numOfTerms = jo["numOfTerms"]  as Int
    self.escrow = jo["escrow"] as Double
    self.extra = jo["extra"] as Double
    self.expenses = jo["expenses"] as Double
    self.rent = jo["rent"] as Double
    return true;

  } else {
    return false
  }
}
...
```

5. Implement the save() method that persists the
    RentalProperty instance in storage, as shown in
    Listing 5-10.

Listing 5-10. Saving RentalProperty Object

```
class RentalProperty {
  ...
  func save() -> Bool {
    var jo : [NSObject : AnyObject] = [
    "purchasePrice": purchasePrice,
    "loanAmt" : loanAmt,
    "interestRate" : interestRate,
    "numOfTerms" : Double(numOfTerms),
    "escrow" : escrow,
    "extra" : extra,
    "expenses" : expenses,
    "rent" : rent]

    return self.saveUserdefault(jo, forKey: MyStatic.KEY_PROPERTY)
  }
  ...
```

6. Implement the getSavedAmortization() and
    saveAmortization() methods to retrieve and save the
    amortization schedule array, as shown in Listing 5-11.

Listing 5-11. Retrieve Amortization Schedule Array from Persistent Storage

```
class RentalProperty {
  ...
  private func getAmortizationPersistentKey() -> String {
    var aKey = String(format: "%.2f-%.3f-%d-%.2f-%.2f", self.loanAmt,
    self.interestRate, self.numOfTerms, self.escrow, self.extra);
    return aKey;
  }
```

```
func getSavedAmortization() -> NSArray? {
  var savedKey = retrieveUserdefault(MyStatic.KEY_AMO_SAVED) as String?
  var aKey = self.getAmortizationPersistentKey()
  if let str = savedKey {
    if(str.utf16Count > 0 && str == aKey) {
      var jo = retrieveUserdefault(str) as NSArray?
      return jo
    }
  }
  return nil
}

func saveAmortization(data: NSArray) -> Bool {
  var aKey = self.getAmortizationPersistentKey()
  saveUserdefault(aKey, forKey: MyStatic.KEY_AMO_SAVED)
  return saveUserdefault(data, forKey: aKey)
}
...
```

EditTextViewController

The purpose of this controller is to prompt users to enter text and return the user input to its presenting view controller. Although this `EditTextView` storyboard scene looks simple, it demonstrates a frequent usage in iOS apps: the presenting view controller passes data to the presented view controller (see Chapter 3). Also, frequently, the presented view controller returns data to the presenting view controller, introduced next.

Return Data to the Presenting View Controller

To return data to the presenting view controller, the iOS SDK uses a callback to the delegate pattern in many system classes. You will implement the same design pattern for your purposes. Do the following:

1. Define the `EditTextViewControllerDelegate` delegate protocol, as shown in Listing 5-12.

    a. Conventionally, you declare this protocol in the same Swift file where the presented view controller is declared.

    b. Conventionally, the first argument in the callback methods are the presented view controller.

Listing 5-12. The Callback Protocol in EditTextViewController.swift File

```
// Callback protocol
protocol EditTextViewControllerDelegate {
  func onTextEditSaved(vc: EditTextViewController, data: String);
  func onTextEditCanceled(vc: EditTextViewController);
}

class EditTextViewController : UIViewController, UITextFieldDelegate {
  ...
```

    2.   Implement the presented view controller, as shown in
        Listing 5-13.

        a.   Implement stored properties to receive data
            from the presenting view controller including the
            delegate.

        b.   To return the data to the presenting view controller,
            use the delegate stored property to deliver the
            return data via the callback method. The doSave()
            code returns the text entered in the UITextField
            when the Save button is clicked.

Listing 5-13. Java Fields to Swift Stored Properties

```
class EditTextViewController : ... {
  ...
  // a.
  var tag: NSIndexPath!
  var header = ""
  var text = ""
  var delegate: EditTextViewControllerDelegate?
  ...
  @IBAction func doSave(sender: AnyObject) {
    var returnText = self.mEditText.text
    if(delegate != nil) {
      // b. return data to the delegate
      delegate!.onTextEditSaved(self, data: returnText)
    }
  }

  @IBAction func doCancel(sender: AnyObject) {
    if(delegate != nil) {
      delegate!.onTextEditCanceled(self)
    }
    ...
```

3. Listing 5-14 depicts the code in
    `RentalPropertyViewController` using
    `EditTextViewController` to get user inputs.

    a. Declare that you are implementing the
        `EditTextViewControllerDelegate` protocol.

    b. Assign itself to be the callback delegate, the
        same way as you pass data to the presented view
        controller. (See Chapter 3.)

    c. Implement the `EditTextViewControllerDelegate`
        callback methods to receive the data returned from
        the presented view controller.

Listing 5-14. Presenting ViewController

```
// 3a implement protocol
class RentalPropertyViewController : UITableViewController,
EditTextViewControllerDelegate  {
  ...
  // You will often want to do a little preparation before segue navigation
  override func prepareForSegue(segue: UIStoryboardSegue,
  sender: AnyObject?) {
    var identifier = segue.identifier
    if identifier == "EditText" {
      var indexPath = sender as NSIndexPath

      var presentedVc = (segue.destinationViewController as
      UINavigationController).topViewController as EditTextViewController
      var cell = tableView.cellForRowAtIndexPath(indexPath)!

      presentedVc.tag = indexPath
      presentedVc.header = cell.textLabel!.text!
      presentedVc.text = cell.detailTextLabel!.text!

      // 3b. assign self to the callback
      presentedVc.delegate = self
    } else { // AmortizationTable segue
      var toFrag = segue.destinationViewController as
      AmortizationViewController
      toFrag.monthlyTerms = sender as NSArray // TODO: a temp
      compilation error
    }
  }
```

```
// 3c. delegate protocol to receive data via callback from presented VC
func onTextEditSaved(vc: EditTextViewController, data: String) {
  self.dismissViewControllerAnimated(true, completion: nil)
  // TODO: use data
}

func onTextEditCanceled(vc: EditTextViewController) {
  self.dismissViewControllerAnimated(true, completion: nil)
}
...
}
```

Handle Soft Keyboard

The rest of the code in EditTextViewController primarily handles a soft keyboard, aka on-screen keyboard. On iOS, you should use NSNotificationCenter to detect the keyboard shown or hidden and update the widget positions accordingly to accommodate the soft keyboard size. Listing 5-15 shows the completed EditTextViewController class implementation, including how to handle the soft keyboard.

1. In viewDidLoad(), register the keyboard notification callback.

2. Remove the notification callback before the view disappears.

3. Shift the UITextField up or down according to the keyboard shown or hidden by updating NSLayoutConstraint.

4. Use UITextField.becomeFirstResponder to show a soft keyboard programmatically.

Listing 5-15. EditTextViewController Completed Code

```
class EditTextViewController : UIViewController, UITextFieldDelegate {

  @IBOutlet weak var bottomConstraint: NSLayoutConstraint!
  @IBOutlet weak var mEditText: UITextField!

  var tag : NSIndexPath!
  var header = ""
  var text = ""
  var delegate: EditTextViewControllerDelegate!
```

```
override func viewDidLoad() {
  super.viewDidLoad()
  self.navigationItem.title = self.header
  mEditText.text = self.text

// 1. Register keyboard shown notification
  NSNotificationCenter.defaultCenter().addObserver(self,
    selector: "keyboardAppeared:",
    name: UIKeyboardDidShowNotification, object: nil)
}

override func viewDidAppear(animated: Bool) {
  super.viewDidAppear(animated)
  showKeyboard()
}

override func viewWillDisappear(animated: Bool) {
  super.viewWillDisappear(animated)
}

override func viewDidDisappear(animated: Bool) {
  super.viewDidDisappear(animated)
  // 2. Remove keyboard notification
  NSNotificationCenter.defaultCenter().removeObserver(self,
    name: UIKeyboardDidShowNotification, object: nil)
}

@IBAction func doSave(sender: AnyObject) {
  var returnText = self.mEditText.text
  if(delegate != nil) {
    delegate.onTextEditSaved(self, data: returnText)
  }
}

@IBAction func doCancel(sender: AnyObject) {
  if(delegate != nil) {
    delegate.onTextEditCanceled(self)
  }
}

// 3. shift the text field up by changing the autolayout constraint
func keyboardAppeared(notification: NSNotification) {
  println(">>keyboardAppeared")
  var keyboardInfo = notification.userInfo as NSDictionary!
  var kbFrame = keyboardInfo.valueForKey(UIKeyboardFrameBeginUserInfoKey)
    as NSValue
```

```
var kbFrameRect: CGRect = kbFrame.CGRectValue()
var keyboardH = min(kbFrameRect.size.width, kbFrameRect.size.height)
UIView.animateWithDuration(0, animations: { () -> Void in

  if UIDevice.currentDevice().userInterfaceIdiom == .Phone {
    self.bottomConstraint.constant = self.bottomConstraint.constant +
    keyboardH/self.bottomConstraint.multiplier
  }

  }, completion: {(b) -> Void in
    self.mEditText.selectAll(self);
  })
}

// 4. show keyboard
private func showKeyboard() {
  self.mEditText.becomeFirstResponder()
}

private func hideKeyboard() {
  self.mEditText.endEditing(true)
  }
}
```

RentalPropertyViewController

When the app is launched, this is the first content view. The purpose of this view controller is to collect user input and present the amortization schedule.

Listing 5-16 shows the typical ViewController life-cycle methods and UI code.

1. You don't have to implement all the view life-cycle methods. (See Chapter 3 for details.)

    a. Call viewDidLoad() only once. Use it for initialization code.

    b. The viewDidAppear() method is called every time the view appears.

    c. Don't forget call super().

2. Implement the TableView data source for rendering the TableView (see Chapter 3 for details).

3. When user selects each table row, present
    EditTextViewController for editing the text.

    a. Use a Manual Segue to present the
        EditTextViewController.

    b. Pass the current value to the presented view
        controller (see Chapter 3).

    c. To use the data from EditTextViewController,
        implement the EditTextViewControllerDelegate.
        onTextEditSaved(...) method.

Listing 5-16. RentalPropertyViewController Completed Implementation

```
import UIKit

class RentalPropertyViewController : UITableViewController,
EditTextViewControllerDelegate  {
  ...
  var _property = RentalProperty.sharedInstance()
  var _savedAmortization: NSArray?

  // 1a. Lifecycle callback
  override func viewDidLoad() {
    super.viewDidLoad()
    _property.load();
  }

  // 1b. Lifecycle callback
  override func viewDidAppear(animated: Bool) {
    super.viewDidAppear(animated)
    self.navigationItem.title = "Property"
  }

  // button action handle
  @IBAction func doSchedule(sender: AnyObject) {
      // TODO
  }

  // 2. implement tableview datasource
  override func numberOfSectionsInTableView(tableView: UITableView) -> Int {
    return 2    // 2a.
  }
```

```swift
// 2b.
override func tableView(tableView: UITableView, titleForHeaderInSection
section: Int) -> String? {
  if section == 0 {
    return NSLocalizedString("mortgage", comment: "")
  } else {
    return NSLocalizedString("operations", comment: "")
  }
}

// 2c
override func tableView(tableView: UITableView, numberOfRowsInSection
section: Int) -> Int {
  if section == 0 {
    return 7
  } else {
    return 2
  }
}

// 2d
override func tableView(tableView: UITableView, cellForRowAtIndexPath
indexPath: NSIndexPath) -> UITableViewCell {
  var cell = tableView.dequeueReusableCellWithIdentifier("aCell",
  forIndexPath: indexPath) as UITableViewCell
  var textLabel = cell.textLabel!
  var detailTextLabel = cell.detailTextLabel!

  var pos = (indexPath.section, indexPath.row)

  switch (pos) {
  case (0, 0):
    textLabel.text = NSLocalizedString("purchasePrice", comment: "")
    detailTextLabel.text = NSString(format: "%.0f", _property.
    purchasePrice);
  case (0, 1):
    textLabel.text = NSLocalizedString("downPayment", comment: "")

    if (_property.purchasePrice > 0) {
      var down = (1 - _property.loanAmt / _property.purchasePrice) * 100.0;
      detailTextLabel.text = NSString(format: "%.0f", down);

      if (_property.loanAmt == 0 && down > 0) {
        _property.loanAmt = _property.purchasePrice * (1 - down / 100.0);
      }
    } else {
      detailTextLabel.text = "0";
    }
```

```
case (0, 2):
  textLabel.text = NSLocalizedString("loanAmount", comment: "")
  detailTextLabel.text = NSString(format: "%.2f", _property.loanAmt)
case (0, 3):
  textLabel.text = NSLocalizedString("interestRate", comment: "")
  detailTextLabel.text = NSString(format: "%.3f", _property.
  interestRate)
case (0, 4):
  textLabel.text = NSLocalizedString("mortgageTerm", comment: "")
  detailTextLabel.text = NSString(format: "%d", _property.numOfTerms)
case (0, 5):
  textLabel.text = NSLocalizedString("escrowAmount", comment: "")
  detailTextLabel.text = NSString(format: "%.0f", _property.escrow)
case (0, 6):
  textLabel.text = NSLocalizedString("extraPayment", comment: "")
  detailTextLabel.text = NSString(format: "%.0f", _property.escrow);
case (1, 0):
  textLabel.text = NSLocalizedString("expenses", comment: "")
  detailTextLabel.text = NSString(format: "%.0f", _property.expenses);
case (1, 1):
  textLabel.text = NSLocalizedString("rent", comment: "")
  detailTextLabel.text = NSString(format: "%.0f", _property.rent);

default:
  break;
}

return cell
}

// tableView delegate
override func tableView(tableView: UITableView, didSelectRowAtIndexPath
indexPath: NSIndexPath) {
  // 3a.
  self.performSegueWithIdentifier("EditText", sender: indexPath)
}

// You will often want to do a little preparation before segue navigation
override func prepareForSegue(segue: UIStoryboardSegue, sender: AnyObject?) {
  var identifier = segue.identifier
  if identifier == "EditText" {
    var indexPath = sender as NSIndexPath

    var presentedVc = (segue.destinationViewController as
    UINavigationController).topViewController as EditTextViewController
    var cell = tableView.cellForRowAtIndexPath(indexPath)!
```

```
  // 3b.
  presentedVc.tag = indexPath
  presentedVc.header = cell.textLabel!.text!
  presentedVc.text = cell.detailTextLabel!.text!
  presentedVc.delegate = self
} else { // AmortizationTable segue
  // 4e.
  // TODO: coming next
  }
}

// 3c. delegate protocol to receive data from presented VC
func onTextEditSaved(vc: EditTextViewController, data: String) {
  self.dismissViewControllerAnimated(true, completion: nil)

  switch (vc.tag.section, vc.tag.row) {
  case (0,0):
    _property.purchasePrice = (data as NSString).doubleValue;
    var indexPath = NSIndexPath(forRow: 0, inSection: 0)
    var percent = tableView.cellForRowAtIndexPath(indexPath)!.
    detailTextLabel!.text!
    var down = (percent as NSString).doubleValue
    if (_property.purchasePrice > 0 && _property.loanAmt == 0 && down > 0) {
      _property.loanAmt = _property.purchasePrice * (1 - down / 100.0)
    }

    break;
  case (0,1):
    var percentage = (data as NSString).doubleValue / 100.0;
    _property.loanAmt = _property.purchasePrice * (1 - percentage);
    break;
  case (0,2):
    _property.loanAmt = (data as NSString).doubleValue;
    break;
  case (0,3):
    _property.interestRate = (data as NSString).doubleValue;
    break;
  case (0,4):
    _property.numOfTerms = (data as NSString).integerValue;
    break;
  case (0,5):
    _property.escrow = (data as NSString).doubleValue;
    break;
  case (0,6):
    _property.extra = (data as NSString).doubleValue;
    break;
  case (1,0):
    _property.expenses = (data as NSString).doubleValue;
    break;
```

```
  case (1,1):
    _property.rent = (data as NSString).doubleValue;
    break;

  default:
    break;
  }
  tableView.reloadData()
  _property.save();
}

func onTextEditCanceled(vc: EditTextViewController) {
  self.dismissViewControllerAnimated(true, completion: nil)
}
}
```

4. When the Schedule `UIBarButtonItem` is selected,
    the IBAction `doAmortization()` method does the
    following (see Listing 5-17):

    a. Check whether the amortization schedule is already
        saved locally.

    b. To get data from a remote RESTFul service, use
        `NSURLConnection.sendAsynchronousRequest`.

    c. Save the results from the remote service.

    d. Use a Manual Segue to present
        `AmortizationViewController`, which will render the
        schedules in it in content view.

    e. Pass the amortized monthly terms to the presented
        view controller (see Chapter 3).

    f. Handle errors for remote service calls (see
        `UIAlertController` in Chapter 3 for details).

Listing 5-17. doAmortization(...)

```
class RentalPropertyViewController : ... {
  ...
  // define constants
  struct MyStatic {
    private static let URL_service_tmpl = "http://www.pdachoice.com/ras/
    service/amortization?loan=%.2f&rate=%.3f&terms=%d&extra=%.2f&escrow=%.2f"
    private static let KEY_DATA = "data"
    private static let KEY_RC = "rc"
    private static let KEY_ERROR = "error"
  }
```

```
// button action handle
@IBAction func doSchedule(sender: AnyObject) {

  // 4a
  _savedAmortization = _property.getSavedAmortization();
  if (_savedAmortization != nil) {
    performSegueWithIdentifier("AmortizationTable",
    sender: _savedAmortization!)
  } else {
    // 4b
    var url = NSString(format: MyStatic.URL_service_tmpl,
    _property.loanAmt, _property.interestRate, _property.numOfTerms,
    _property.extra, _property.escrow)
    UIApplication.sharedApplication().networkActivityIndicatorVisible = true

    var urlRequest = NSMutableURLRequest(URL: NSURL(string: url)!)
    urlRequest.HTTPMethod = "GET"
    urlRequest.setValue("text/html",forHTTPHeaderField: "accept")
    NSURLConnection.sendAsynchronousRequest(urlRequest, queue:
    NSOperationQueue.mainQueue(),
      completionHandler: {(resp: NSURLResponse!, data: NSData!,
      error: NSError!) -> Void in
        NSURLConnection.sendAsynchronousRequest(urlRequest, queue:
        NSOperationQueue.mainQueue(),
          completionHandler: {(resp: NSURLResponse!, data: NSData!,
          error: NSError!) -> Void in
            UIApplication.sharedApplication().
            networkActivityIndicatorVisible = false
            var errMsg: String?
            if error == nil {
              var statusCode = (resp as NSHTTPURLResponse).statusCode
              if(statusCode == 200) {
                var str = NSString(data: data, encoding:
                NSUTF8StringEncoding)
                var parseErr: NSError?
                var json = NSJSONSerialization.JSONObjectWithData(data,
                options: NSJSONReadingOptions.AllowFragments,
                error: &parseErr) as NSArray?
                if parseErr == nil {
                  // 4c. save
                  self._property.saveAmortization(json!)
                  // 4d. segue navigation
                  self.performSegueWithIdentifier("AmortizationTable",
                  sender: json!)
                  return
                } else {
                  errMsg = parseErr?.debugDescription
                }
```

```
              } else {
                errMsg = "HTTP RC: \(statusCode)"
              }
            } else {
              errMsg = error.debugDescription
            }

            // 4f. simple error handling
            var alert = UIAlertController(title: "Error", message: errMsg,
            preferredStyle: UIAlertControllerStyle.Alert)
            var actionCancel = UIAlertAction(title: "Cancel",
            style: UIAlertActionStyle.Cancel,
              handler: {action in
                // do nothing
            })
            alert.addAction(actionCancel)
            self.presentViewController(alert, animated: true,
            completion: nil)
        })
      })
    }
  }

  override func prepareForSegue(segue: UIStoryboardSegue, sender: AnyObject?) {
    var identifier = segue.identifier
    if identifier == "EditText" {
      // 3b.
      ...
    } else { // AmortizationTable segue
      // 4e.
      var toVc = segue.destinationViewController as
      AmortizationViewController
      toVc.monthlyTerms = sender as NSArray // a temp error to be fixed next
    }
  }
...
```

You should get a temporary compilation error in 4e because you haven't defined the monthlyTerms stored properties yet. You will do that next.

AmortizationViewController

Let's move on to `AmortizationViewController`. The sole purpose of this view is to render the amortization items in a `TableView`. Listing 5-18 shows the completed implementation.

1. The amortization schedule results are obtained and passed by the presenting view controller, `RentalPropertyViewController` (Listing 5-17 step 4b and 4f).

2. Implement the `UITableViewDataSource` methods (see Chapter 3).

3. When a particular month is selected, present the monthly details in `MonthlyTermViewController` using a segue navigation.

4. Pass the monthly term data to the presented view controller.

Listing 5-18. AmortizationViewController Class, Completed Code

```
import UIKit
class AmortizationViewController: UITableViewController {

  // 1. From the presenting view controller
  var monthlyTerms: NSArray!

  override func viewDidLoad() {
    super.viewDidLoad()
  }

  override func tableView(tableView: UITableView, numberOfRowsInSection
  section: Int) -> Int {
    return monthlyTerms.count
  }

  override func tableView(tableView: UITableView, cellForRowAtIndexPath
  indexPath: NSIndexPath) -> UITableViewCell {

    var cell = tableView.dequeueReusableCellWithIdentifier("aCell") as
    UITableViewCell!
    var textLabel = cell.textLabel!
    var detailTextLabel = cell.detailTextLabel!
    var pos = indexPath.row
    var monthlyTerm = monthlyTerms[pos] as NSDictionary
```

```
    var pmtNo = monthlyTerm["pmtNo"] as Int
    var balance0 = monthlyTerm["balance0"] as Double
    textLabel.text = NSString(format: "%d\t $%.2f", pmtNo, balance0)

    var interest = monthlyTerm["interest"] as Double
    var principal = monthlyTerm["principal"] as Double

    var property = RentalProperty.sharedInstance();
    var invested = property.purchasePrice - property.loanAmt + (property.
    extra * Double(pmtNo))
    var net = property.rent - property.escrow - interest - property.expenses
    var roi = net * 12 / invested

    detailTextLabel.text = NSString(format: "Interest: %.2f\tPrincipal:
    %.2f\t ROI: %.2f", interest, principal, roi * 100);

    return cell
}

override func viewDidAppear(animated: Bool) {
  super.viewDidAppear(animated)
  self.navigationItem.title = NSLocalizedString("label_Amortization",
  comment: "")
}

override func tableView(tableView: UITableView, didSelectRowAtIndexPath
indexPath: NSIndexPath) {
    // 3. Present MonthlyTerm view controller
    self.performSegueWithIdentifier("MonthlyTerm", sender: indexPath)
}

override func prepareForSegue(segue: UIStoryboardSegue, sender:
AnyObject?) {
  var vc = segue.destinationViewController as MonthlyTermViewController
  // 4. Pass data to the presented view controller
  var row = (sender! as NSIndexPath).row
  vc.monthlyTerm = monthlyTerms[row] as NSDictionary // TODO: a temp error
}
}
```

This completes the whole AmortizationViewController Swift class
implementation, with a temporarily compilation error in step 4. You will
define the monthlyTerm stored property next.

MonthlyTermViewController

Let's move on to `MonthlyTermViewController`. It renders the detailed information for the selected month, as shown in Listing 5-19.

1. The monthlyTerm data is obtained from the presenting view controller, AmortizationViewController (Listing 5-18 step 4).

2. Fill the IBOutlet UI widgets with data in the selected monthlyTerm stored property.

Listing 5-19. AmortizationViewController Class Completed Code

```
import UIKit
class MonthlyTermViewController : UITableViewController {

  @IBOutlet weak var mPaymentNo: UILabel!
  @IBOutlet weak var mTotalPmt: UILabel!
  @IBOutlet weak var mPrincipal: UILabel!
  @IBOutlet weak var mInterest: UILabel!
  @IBOutlet weak var mEscrow: UILabel!
  @IBOutlet weak var mAddlPmt: UILabel!
  @IBOutlet weak var mBalance: UILabel!
  @IBOutlet weak var mEquity: UILabel!
  @IBOutlet weak var mCashInvested: UILabel!
  @IBOutlet weak var mRoi: UILabel!

  // 1. From the presenting view controller
  var monthlyTerm: NSDictionary!

  override func viewDidLoad() {
    super.viewDidLoad()

    // 3. Fill the widget with data before view appears.
    var principal = self.monthlyTerm["principal"] as Double
    var interest = self.monthlyTerm["interest"] as Double
    var escrow = self.monthlyTerm["escrow"] as Double
    var extra = self.monthlyTerm["extra"] as Double
    var balance = (self.monthlyTerm["balance0"] as Double) - principal
    var paymentPeriod = self.monthlyTerm["pmtNo"] as Int
    var totalPmt = principal + interest + escrow + extra
    self.mTotalPmt.text = NSString(format: "$%.2f", totalPmt)
    self.mPaymentNo.text = NSString(format: "No. %d", paymentPeriod)
    self.mPrincipal.text = NSString(format: "$%.2f", principal)
    self.mInterest.text = NSString(format: "$%.2f", interest)
    self.mEscrow.text = NSString(format: "$%.2f", escrow)
    self.mAddlPmt.text = NSString(format: "$%.2f", extra)
    self.mBalance.text = NSString(format: "$%.2f", balance)
```

```swift
        var property = RentalProperty.sharedInstance();
        var invested = property.purchasePrice - property.loanAmt +
        (property.extra * Double(paymentPeriod))
        var net = property.rent - escrow - interest - property.expenses;
        var roi = net * 12 / invested

        self.mEquity.text = NSString(format: "$%.2f", property.purchasePrice -
        balance)
        self.mCashInvested.text = NSString(format: "$%.2f", invested)
        self.mRoi.text = NSString(format: "%.2f%% ($%.2f/mo)", roi * 100, net)
    }
}
```

This completes the whole `MonthlyTermViewController` Swift class implementation.

All the class translations are completed. Build and run the iOS RentalROI app and do some testing. Your app should look like Figure 5-1.

Summary

This chapter showed you how to apply the individual topics introduced in Chapters 3 and 4—such as creating master list details, creating drill-down navigation, exchanging data between view controllers, using basic UI widgets, saving data, and using remote services—all in one simple and meaningful app.

Although the RentalROI app is not complicated enough to show you all the topics in this book, the general iOS app development steps remain the same. You started with the Xcode storyboard and created view controllers to pair with the storyboard scenes. Then, you implemented storyboard segues to connect the view controller together. The result was a set of connected view controllers. With the storyboard in place, you started following the use case paths and discovering the business objects and methods, and the dots started connecting to each other.

When you encounter platform-specific SDK or topics, use this book's table of contents to find the instructions that will guide you through the iOS SDK.

Chapter 6

Bonus Chapter: Hybrid Apps

For serious web developers using JavaScript to create interactive web apps, UIWebView provides a seamless way to transfer those skills to creating mobile apps. UIWebView also allows native code to interface with the JavaScript that is loaded with the web page. Both iOS and Android inject JavaScript code from the native code into the embedded browser. Web developers normally think it is easier to use their familiar development skills to create their web apps, but using this hybrid approach opens up a different way to create mobile apps.

The so-called hybrid approach has gained a bit of attraction in recent years; there are many cross-platform compilers aimed at JavaScript developers who want to create mobile apps. To name a few, PhoneGap, Apache Cordova, Titanium, Icenium, Trigger.IO, and so forth, all seem to be doing a good job for the intended purpose.

The key is how to interface the code between JavaScript and native iOS SDK to make it bi-directional. It is relatively easier to have your native iOS code interface with your JavaScript code because this process is well-documented using the existing iOS API. However, how to call iOS code from your JavaScript code doesn't seem to be well-known yet, so I will reveal the secret that's used in those third-party frameworks. The process is actually very easy.

To learn by example, you will be implementing an iOS app that calls functions between your Swift code and your JavaScript code. Figure 6-1 shows the completed iOS app you will be creating.

Figure 6-1. Simple hybrid app screens

This hybrid app performs the following tasks:

- The content is implemented as an HTML page and rendered in an UIWebView that takes up all the space under the iOS-native UINavigationBar.

- To change the image from your iOS code, select the UISegmentedControl.

- To change the image from your JavaScript code, click the <img> element. This also changes the native UISegmentedControl selection.

Follow the usual steps to get started, shown here:

1. Create an iOS project using the Xcode Single View Application template. Name the project HybridApp. You immediately get a storyboard with one ViewController.swift file that pairs with the view controller scene, as shown in Figure 6-2.

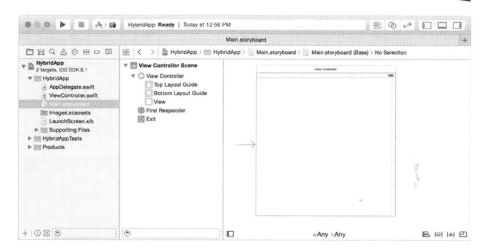

Figure 6-2. Creating an iOS project using the Single View Application template

2. Drag a web view from the Object Library onto the root view in the view controller scene.

    a. Position and size it to take up the whole space.

    b. With the web view selected, select Resolve Auto Layout Issues ➤ Reset to Suggested Constraints to automatically add zero-space constraints to its parent view.

3. With the view controller in the storyboard selected, from the Xcode menu bar, select Editor ➤ Embed In ➤ Navigation Controller. You get a navigation controller scene, a navigation item, and a navigation bar in the view controller scene.

4. With the navigation item selected, drag a segmented control from the Object Library onto the right side of the navigation bar, as shown in Figure 6-3.

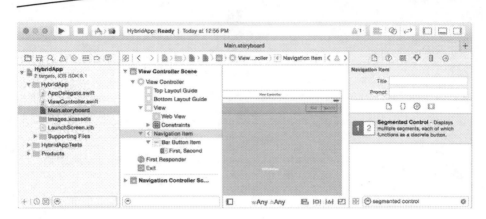

Figure 6-3. Drawing a navigation bar and a segmented control in the right bar button

5. Use the Assistant Editor to connect the following storyboard outlets to your code in `ViewController.swift`. Listing 6-1 depicts the storyboard operations results.

   a. Connect a web view delegate to the `ViewController` class.

   b. Connect a web view referencing outlet to the `ViewController mWebview` stored property.

   c. Connect a segmented control referencing outlet to the `ViewController mSegmentControl` stored property.

   d. Connect a segmented control value changed event to the `ViewController onValueChanged(...)` `IBAction` function.

   e. Declare a `ViewController` that implements `UIWebViewDelegate` protocol. (You will implement the protocol methods later.)

   f. To make sure the previous storyboard tasks are working, you can add a line in `viewDidLoad` and some logging code just to see whether all the outlets are good.

Listing 6-1. Storyboard Outlets in ViewController.swift

```swift
import UIKit

class ViewController: UIViewController, UIWebViewDelegate {

  @IBOutlet weak var mWebview: UIWebView!
  @IBOutlet weak var mSegmentControl: UISegmentedControl!

  override func viewDidLoad() {
    super.viewDidLoad()
    // Do any additional setup after loading the view, typically from a nib.
    mWebview.loadHTMLString("<h1>Hello HybridApp</h1>", baseURL: nil)
  }

  override func didReceiveMemoryWarning() {
    super.didReceiveMemoryWarning()
    // Dispose of any resources that can be recreated.
  }

  @IBAction func onValueChanged(sender: AnyObject) {
    println(">> onValueChanged")
  }

  func webView(webView: UIWebView, shouldStartLoadWithRequest request:
  NSURLRequest, navigationType: UIWebViewNavigationType) -> Bool {

    return true
  }

}
```

Nothing you've done here is new yet. It was the same storyboard tasks as usual. Run and test the HybridApp project. You should see the HybridApp app as shown in Figure 6-4.

Figure 6-4. HybridApp storyboard tasks

Bundle Web Contents

Recall that in the UIWebView code in Chapter 4's Listing 4-18, you used
UIWebView.loadRequest(NSURLRequest) to load the remote URL. You can
bundle the web contents with the iOS app and still use the same API to
load the web contents using a file URL to the bundled local files. Do the
following:

1. Develop your web content as usual. Instead of
    deploying the web content to the web server, bundle
    it in the HybridApp project.

    a. Figure 6-5 shows a simple web content root folder.
        You can organize your web content with subfolders
        like you normally do.

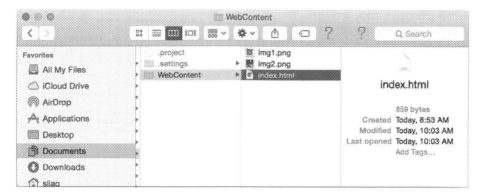

Figure 6-5. HybridApp web content

b.   Listing 6-2 depicts the demo `index.html` file that contains two inline JavaScript functions. You will use them in later sections.

Listing 6-2. The Simple Web content-index.html

```
<!DOCTYPE html>
<html>
<head>
<meta charset="UTF-8">
<script>
   function onClicked() {
      console.log('onClicked');
      var name = document.getElementById('imgId').name;
      // <scheme name> : <hierarchical part> [ ? <query> ] [ # <fragment> ]
      document.location.href = 'uiwebview://onClicked?img=' + name;
   }

   function replaceImg(src) { // to be called from Swift code
      console.log('replaceImg: ' + src);
      document.getElementById('imgId').src = src;
      document.getElementById('imgId').name = src;
   }
</script>

<title>Hybrid App</title>
</head>
<body>
   <div>
     <H1>My Image</H1>
     <img id=imgId src='img0.png' name= 'img0.png' onClick="onClicked();" />
   </div>
</body>
</html>
```

2.   Drag the WebContent root folder from the iOS Finder
to the Xcode HybridApp project.

a.   This is similar to adding image assets to your Xcode
project, but make sure you select Create Folder
Reference to preserve the URL path, as shown in
Figure 6-6.

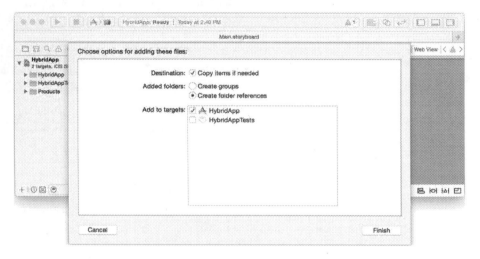

Figure 6-6. Adding web content to the Xcode project

b.   You may directly modify index.html or any web
content in the Xcode editor from now on. For
example, you can remove the <h1> element in the
index.html file using the Xcode editor. Figure 6-7
depicts the results with the WebContent folder in the
HybridApp project.

Figure 6-7. WebContent folder in Xcode

3. Listing 6-3 depicts how to render the local web
    content in UIWebView.

    a. Obtain the file path for the bundled resource using
        NSBundle.pathForResource(...).

    b. You still use the same UIWebView.loadRequest(...)
        method to load the file URL.

Listing 6-3. Load Bundled Web Contents

```
class ViewController: UIViewController, UIWebViewDelegate {

  @IBOutlet weak var mWebview: UIWebView!
  override func viewDidLoad() {
    super.viewDidLoad()
    // Do any additional setup after loading the view, typically from a nib.

    var htmlfile = NSBundle.mainBundle().pathForResource("index", ofType:
    "html", inDirectory: "WebContent")
    var htmlfileUrl = NSURL(fileURLWithPath: htmlfile!)

    // mWebview.loadHTMLString("<h1>Hello HybridApp</h1>", baseURL: nil)
       mWebview.loadRequest(NSURLRequest(URL: htmlfileUrl!))
  }
}
```

You can build and run the iOS HybridApp project to see the bundled web
contents being rendered in offline mode.

Invoke JavaScript Function

To call JavaScript functions from iOS code, you simply inject JavaScript code into UIWebView. The following steps walk you through a typical usage that invokes a JavaScript function from iOS code:

1. You can inject any JavaScript code, including declaring the whole function. Previously in Listing 6-2, the inline replaceImg(src) JavaScript function replaces the src attribute in the <img> DOM element, which you can easily invoke from your native Swift code (see Listing 6-4).

Listing 6-4. The replaceImg(...) JavaScript Function Inline in index.html

```
...
<script>
   ...
   function replaceImg(src) {
      console.log('replaceImg: ' + src);
      document.getElementById('imgId').src = src;
      document.getElementById('imgId').name = src;
   }
   ...
```

2. Listing 6-5 changes the image in UIWebView by invoking the replaceImg(...) JavaScript code. This is achieved by injecting JavaScript into UIWebView using stringByEvaluatingJavaScriptFromString.

Listing 6-5. Inject JavaScript Code into the Embedded Browser, UIWebView

```
class ViewController: UIViewController, UIWebViewDelegate {
  ...
  @IBAction func onValueChanged(sender: AnyObject) {
     var selection = (sender as UISegmentedControl).selectedSegmentIndex
     var img = selection == 0 ? "img0.png" : "img1.png"
     var jsCode = "replaceImg('" + img + "')"  // js: replaceImg('img2.png')
     self.mWebview.stringByEvaluatingJavaScriptFromString(jsCode)
  }
  ...
```

You can build and run the iOS HybridApp project and select the UISegmentedControl to change the image in the UIWebView.

Invoke Native Code

UIWebView goes through the life cycle defined in the UIWebViewDelegate protocol when loading a URL. The following approach intercepts the UIWebView's early life-cycle events and takes the chance to call your Swift code:

1. Previously in Listing 6-2, the `<img>` onClick() event invokes the onClicked() JavaScript function. In the JavaScript code, build a URL request with a custom URI scheme that only your native code understands.

   a. I chose uiwebview as my custom URI scheme name. You can choose any scheme name as long as it is unique and only your native code understands it.

   b. To pass extra data from JavaScript, I chose to use the URI query part.

   c. To dispatch the request to the appropriate native method, I chose to use the URI hierarchical part.

   d. `document.location.href` will start loading the URL, which gives UIWebView a chance to intercept the request via callback. See Listing 6-6.

Listing 6-6. The Simple Web content-index.html

```
<html>
...
<script>
   function onClicked() {
      console.log('onClicked');
      var name = document.getElementById('imgId').name;
      // <scheme name> : <hierarchical part> [ ? <query> ] [ # <fragment> ]
      document.location.href = 'uiwebview://onClicked?img=' + name;
   }
   ...
```

> **Note** URI is defined as consisting of four parts: `<scheme name>` :
> `<hierarchical part>` [? `<query>`] [# `<fragment>`].
> As long as you set them, you will be able to intercept them easily in your native code.

2. Implement the UIWebViewDelegate protocol to intercept the URL request, as shown in Listing 6-7.

    a. Intercept the request by the custom scheme name and return false to stop the page load. You just need to know an action is triggered from JavaScript, but you return true without breaking the real page load request.

    b. Since there is only one interface method, I didn't care that the URI hierarchical part is passed from JavaScript function. If I need to interface with different methods from different JavaScript code, I would use it as the switch-case condition to dispatch calls to appropriate Swift method.

    c. The Swift code updated the segmented control selection and updated the images by calling the existing UISegmentedControl.onValueChanged(...) method discussed previously in Listing 6-5.

Listing 6-7. Intercept the Custom Page Load Request

```
class ViewController: UIViewController, UIWebViewDelegate {
  ...
  let CUSTOM_SCHEME = "uiwebview"
  func webView(webView: UIWebView, shouldStartLoadWithRequest request:
  NSURLRequest, navigationType: UIWebViewNavigationType) -> Bool {
    println(">>shouldStartLoadWithRequest")

    var url = request.URL
    if let scheme = url.scheme {
      if scheme.lowercaseString == CUSTOM_SCHEME {
        var host = url.host // URI  hierarchical part, not used

        var queryString = url.query!
        println("queryString: \(queryString)");

        var img = queryString.componentsSeparatedByString("=")[1]
        var isImg0 = img == "img0.png"
        self.mSegmentControl.selectedSegmentIndex = isImg0 ? 1 : 0
        self.onValueChanged(self.mSegmentControl)

        return false
      }
    }

    return true
  }
```

Build and run HybridApp. You can select the `UISegmentedControl` or click the `<img>` element in the `UIWebView` to change the image in the `UIWebView`.

This completes the bi-directional interface between JavaScript and iOS native code. It is much lighter than those popular cross-platform frameworks and has great extensibility. In most cases, you really don't need those heavy cross-platform frameworks that often offer too many features for your apps.

Index

A, B, C

AppDelegate.swift, 39

D

Dialogs
  IBAction methods, 111
  storyboard, 110
  UIAlertController, 112
  UIPopoverController, 113
    Attributes Inspector, 115
    GreenViewController
      class, 114
    iPad *vs.* iPhone, 116
    mypopover manual
      segue, 115
    storyboard completion, 114
Drilldown patterns
  mobile navigation patterns, 85
  UICollectionView, 92
  UITableViewController, 86
    dequeueReusableCellWith
      Identifier(), 89
    MasterDetail
      storyboard, 88
    table view cell, 87
    UITableView, 91
    UITableViewCell, 92
    UITableViewDataSource, 89
    UITableViewDelegate, 89

E, F

Efficient navigation, 73
Emulator, LessonOne app in, 9

G

Graphical user interface (GUI), 52

H

HelloSwift Xcode project, 12
  class creation
    context menu, 16
    MobileDeveloper class, 16
    stored property, 16
    Swift file template, 15
  command-line tool
    Project Navigator area, 14
    Source Editor area, 14
    template, 13
    utility area, 15
  debugger, 21
  instance, 19
  Programmer protocol, 17
  protocol declaration
    method, 18
    MobileDeveloper
      protocol, 18
HTTP GET method, 182
HTTP POST method, 181
Hybrid approach
  iOS app creation, 225
    Assistant Editor, 228
    Navigation Controller, 227
    Object Library, 227
    screens, 226
    Single View Application
      template, 227
    storyboard tasks, 229
    ViewController.swift, 229

▓ V, W

▓ X, Y, Z

Get the eBook for only $10!

Now you can take the weightless companion with you anywhere, anytime. Your purchase of this book entitles you to 3 electronic versions for only $10.

This Apress title will prove so indispensible that you'll want to carry it with you everywhere, which is why we are offering the eBook in 3 formats for only $10 if you have already purchased the print book.

Convenient and fully searchable, the PDF version enables you to easily find and copy code—or perform examples by quickly toggling between instructions and   applications. The MOBI format is ideal for your Kindle, while the ePUB can be utilized on a variety of mobile devices.

Go to www.apress.com/promo/tendollars to purchase your companion eBook.

<barcode>||| || || ■ |■|||||■||| |■ ||| ||| ■ || ■ ||||||■| ■■ ||| ■ || ■ |||</barcode>

Printed in the United States
By Bookmasters